ALEXANDRA DANILOVA

ALEXANDRA DANILOVA IN "LE BEAU DANUBE"

From the original drawing in sanguine by A. Yakovlev

ALEXANDRA DANILOVA

By
A. E. TWYSDEN

LONDON
C. W. BEAUMONT
75, CHARING CROSS ROAD, LONDON, W.C.2

To
"CHOURA"
with love and profound admiration
from
ELIZABETH

First printed, 1945

Printed in Great Britain by
Wyman & Sons, Limited, London, Fakenham and Reading.

CONTENTS

LIST OF ILLUSTRATIONS

AUTHOR'S PREFACE

HAD it not been for the outbreak of war in 1939 this book would have been achieved by an abler pen than mine, since Mr. Cyril W. Beaumont, the well-known historian of the ballet, had contemplated writing a book on Mlle. Danilova as long ago as 1937. Circumstances prevented his being free for the undertaking until the summer of 1939, when he himself told me that he would like to collect his material during the forthcoming season of the Ballet Russe de Monte Carlo at the Opera House, Covent Garden, in September. That season, however, did not materialise, and although Mlle. Danilova remained in England for some weeks awaiting instructions from the directorate of Universal Art, Inc., she and Mr. Beaumont were never in London at the same time and consequently they failed to meet.

Months passed and the war showed no signs of ending, when one day in Buenos Aires, while discussing ballet and dancers, with Mr. Sol. Hurok, he suddenly remarked: "Why don't you write a book about Danilova?" After some consideration I decided at any rate to make the attempt, feeling that an authentic account of her career would be of definite value to future biographers as well as of interest to the public at large.

To this end I approached Mlle. Danilova with two requests: for permission to write such a book, and for her assistance in the matter. She not only authorised me to attempt an account of her career but most kindly consented to afford me any information that I might need. Hence she herself is responsible for all the essential facts which are recorded in the pages that follow. Further material has been collected from her friends and associates, all of which is duly acknowledged, either in the text itself or in a footnote on the same page. My thanks for their information, as well as for their impressions of Alexandra Danilova and her dancing, are due to Mlles. Felia Doubrovska, Alicia Markova, Maria Bekefi, and Vera Timé; to Mme. Leonide Massine, Georges Balanchine, Anton Dolin, and Igor Schvezov; to Miss Ruth Howard for the loan of reference books; to Mr. and Mrs. Kamin of the Kamin Book Shop for their extreme kindness and encouragement and for the loan of photographs; to Mr.

Anatole Chujoy for much helpful advice and one photograph; to Mlle. Tatiana Chamié for one photograph; and to Miss Janet Roughton and Miss Helen Hirst for so patiently deciphering my handwriting. I desire to record my sincere appreciation of the courtesy of Major the Hon. Maurice Baring in according me permission to quote from his book, *The Russian People*. I am also indebted to Mr. S. Hurok and to the directorate of the Ballet Russe de Monte Carlo who have aided me, in every way, to become acquainted with ballet in all its aspects.

Last, but not least, I owe a great deal to Alexandra Danilova herself, who has accorded me so much of her valuable time, and to whose talent this book is a humble offering.

A. E. TWYSDEN

INTRODUCTION

MANY of my friends have been asking me to write a book about myself, telling all about the Theatre School in Russia, as I am the only *ballerina* trained there who is dancing abroad at the present time. All those who were in the School with me are dancing in Russia now. One day I will perhaps write such a book, but at the moment, with hard work and constant travelling, it is simply impossible to do so.

Last year Miss Twysden told me that she wanted to write about me and asked me if I would give her all details so that it might be a true account. I gladly did so and now here is a short story of myself. It tells how I was trained in the great Russian tradition in the Theatre School of Petrograd (Leningrad) through all the troubled time of the Revolution, how I went abroad, how I joined the Diaghilev Company, and so on right up to the present day.

All of this I hope will be of interest to my dear Public who visit the Ballet.

(Signed) ALEXANDRA DANILOVA

Chapter I

YEARS OF CHILDHOOD

NOT far from the Capital City of Russia—now called Leningrad, but better known to the world in general as St. Petersburg, or Petrograd—there lies a town which in many respects bears the same relationship to its larger neighbour that Versailles does to Paris. Peterhov, for such is its name, consisted in pre-Revolutionary times of a huge palace, the houses of the Court circle, and the barracks of the Imperial Guard, while its gardens and fountains, in much the same style as those of Versailles, were very nearly as famous as those of Louis XIV, though by no means as easy of access to the wandering tourist.

It was here, some half-dozen years before the first World War, on November 20th, that there was born to Dionis Danilov and his wife Clavdia a second daughter, their first, Helen, being then nearly two years old; this second baby was in due time baptised in the Church of the Grenadier Guards at Peterhov and given the name of Alexandra.

Little Alexandra Dionisevna Danilova, or "Choura" (pronounced "Shura") as she was always called, seems to have been a normal baby and to have lived a quiet and sheltered existence until she reached the age of two, when a tragedy occurred which altered the whole course of her life. Her father caught a chill while out hunting, became seriously ill, and finally died of pneumonia, while shortly afterwards his wife, worn out with nursing him, died also, leaving their two little daughters to the care of their grandmother. All might still have been well for the orphans had not the grandmother, in her turn, died suddenly when the younger girl was three years old, leaving the two children alone once more, and this time without any near relatives.

Now it was Alexandra's godmother, Mme. Molvo, who came to the rescue. She had a large country house not far from Peterhov, and she took both the children there to live with her. Here Helen was fairly happy, but the younger sister was very miserable, and so was pleased, rather than otherwise, when her godmother informed her, some months later, that a lady was coming to see her who would shortly take her away and be a second mother to her. This lady, Mme. Lydia Gotovzeva, had recently lost a child of her own about the same age, and was determined to adopt little Choura, now that she was left so alone in the world, and she told the child to regard her as an aunt and to call her by that name.

Alexandra Danilova well remembers the day when, being then four years old, she was taken to her new home in St. Petersburg, and it is here that we first get a clear picture of her in her childhood. She relates how, as soon as the door of the apartment was opened, three dogs—a St. Bernard, a setter, and a pug—rushed at her, barking loudly. Not being accustomed to dogs she was absolutely terrified, so the butler, seeing how the animals towered above her (she was tiny even for her years), lifted her up on a chair where she stood, and, to quote her own words: "I cried and cried for I was so very frightened." The combined noise of crying child and barking dogs, however, brought assistance, and she was carried away to be caressed and comforted. Despite this inauspicious beginning her life with her adopted family was destined to be very happy, and she even managed within a short time to make friends with the pug "Touzik", and with another dog, a Spitz, which was later added to the pack. Horses also attracted her and to be allowed to visit the stables was a joy, although she was never taught to ride, as it was not then considered suitable for children to ride in the city.

Mme. Gotovzeva took the greatest care of the child, bringing her up as though she were in very fact her own daughter, and engaging a German lady to look after her, for at that time foreign governesses were all the rage in St. Petersburg. However, the new member of the family was not given much time to settle down and feel at home, for as soon as summer arrived her aunt decided to spend two or three months in Caucasia, which involved a three-days' journey, the train being quite a new experience for Choura, and one which she enjoyed and which made her very hungry, for she remembers "eating all the time."

Their destination was Kislauvodsk, or "Sour Waters," a fashionable watering place which remained for ever in the child's memory, not only for its beauty (she said in later years that she had never seen any other place quite so beautiful), but because of the escapades in which she indulged and the consequent scrapes she got into. The town was full of excellent hotels and in the centre was the Spa which was built with a gallery looking on to the Park, and here the people wandered up and down at about eleven in the morning and drank the waters, after which they would walk into the Park to a little café where an orchestra played, and there they would sit until lunch-time.

The Park itself was enormous, and that part nearest the Spa was formally laid out with lawns and flower-beds, but it was necessary to walk an hour before reaching the rose garden, where little fountains played and sparkled amongst the blossoms. This was one of the sights of the town. Quite near this charming spot was the Children's Playground, while further off were the Red Rocks where there was a much-frequented restaurant, and from here the Park grew wilder and wilder until it reached the Blue Mountains which were more than an hour's ride away.

Alexandra Danilova naturally spent most of her time in the Playground where everything possible in the way of swings and games was provided for the children, with special attendants in charge so that they should not get into mischief. Here the children were taken in the afternoons by their governesses, who sat together and watched their charges at play, and it was there that Choura quite unconsciously gave her aunt a dreadful fright. One afternoon she was playing as usual with the other children when something distracted the attention of her governess, who moved away from the spot for a short time, and when she returned she could not see the child anywhere. She searched wildly without result and finally returned to the hotel and told Mme. Gotovzeva what had happened. She, poor lady, quite distraught, and believing that the little girl had been stolen, informed the police; in the meantime, however, the cause of all the trouble was enjoying herself very much picnicking with some other children in the mountains!

It so happened that an excursion had been arranged for some of the children from the Playground, and of this her aunt knew nothing, but Choura, finding that her playmates were going out, quite naturally went with them without for one moment thinking that she was doing wrong. The party left about three o'clock in the afternoon, and returned at seven. All the other children's parents and governesses were there to meet them, but since there was no one for Choura, the authorities telephoned to the hotel, and the search was ended. She had much enjoyed her picnic and was quite unable to understand why her aunt was in tears, for she had only done just the same as her companions.

This affair had unforeseen consequences, however, for a General who aspired to the hand of Mme. Gotovzeva was so foolish as to suggest that the child should be beaten as a punishment for causing her aunt such distress, and Choura, highly indignant at the idea, never forgave its originator, hence when, some time later, her aunt asked her if she would like him for a new father, she cried out in horror: "No! No! If you give him to me, I will run away!" And so the matter went no further.

Nevertheless, her habit of disappearing at any moment was no joke, and eventually her unfortunate governess dared not take her eyes off her for one moment or she would be out of sight, but this was not until after her second adventure which occurred in the hotel lounge. A lady whom she did not know saw her wandering about by herself and spoke to her. Choura, who was not shy, answered quite happily, and in the end the lady asked her what she would like to do, and, having heard a lot of discussion about the cinema, the child answered that she would like to go to the "movies," and having got there, fell fast asleep. About an hour later she awoke, and remarking: I must go home now, thank you," departed, not having found the cinema of much interest after all! This time her aunt was seriously alarmed, gave her story books about children being stolen by gypsies, and had her watched more carefully than ever, though the child does not seem ever to have been convinced of the danger of talking to strangers. The trouble was that being so tiny and pretty with her long curly hair, she attracted attention everywhere, and when spoken to was so naive in her responses as to be extremely amusing to her interlocutors.

Another expedition which she made, but this time quite correctly in company with her aunt, left a great impression on the child's mind. It was to the "Castle of Love and Betrayal" that she went—a castle, then converted into a restaurant, which had once been the scene of a distressing tragedy. The castle stood on the top of a precipice from which a young couple, forbidden to marry, had decided to leap. As they stood there,

THEATRE STREET SHOWING THE BALLET SCHOOL

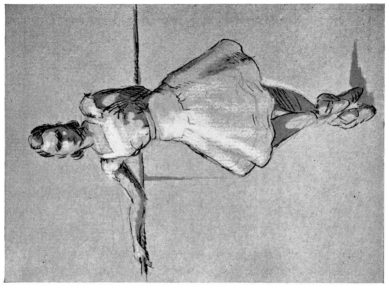

UNIFORM WORN BY PUPILS OF THE IMPERIAL BALLET SCHOOL, ST. PETERSBURG

Dancing Dress

House Dress

the man told the girl to leap first and he would follow. She leapt, but his nerve failed him and he remained alive.

But soon all the beauty and tragedy of Caucasia were but memories, for autumn came and with it the return to St. Petersburg, when life once more took on its customary shape and normal routine. At eight o'clock every morning her governess would wake her and supervise her efforts to wash and dress herself, and then, this ritual completed, she would take her to the dining-room to breakfast with the family, for in Russia then, as in France to this day, there were no nursery meals, and children were expected to behave themselves properly, keep silence in the presence of their elders, and listen to the conversation. This habit has many advantages, for the child, when growing up, has no fear of strangers and is perfectly able to conduct a polite conversation with any guest who may be present.

After breakfast came lessons which lasted until it was time for lunch at one o'clock. Afterwards there was a walk with Fräulein, or a drive, or a shopping expedition with her aunt, which last Choura dearly loved, for she was fussy about her clothes and very particular as to the way in which she was dressed! Mme. Gotovzeva was always much amused by her very definite likes and dislikes and never bought her a dress which displeased her, and sometimes she would also buy her other things to which she had taken a fancy. Once Choura longed for a pair of shoes with pom-poms on the toes, and one day when a red dress had been bought for her she saw just such a pair in red also, and cried out: "Oh, please, please buy them for me to wear with the frock," and the shoes were bought.

However, she did not always get her own way, for some years later, when Choura was seven, she was promoted from socks to stockings, and watched with interest while her aunt inspected some in lisle and some in cotton, and then put the totally unexpected question, "Why not silk?" Now at that time silk stockings were not worn by ladies, except in the evenings, and her aunt exclaimed in horror: "Why, where have you seen silk stockings?" To which Choura replied: "Oh, your maid wears them when she goes out."

"You are not a maid, but a lady," was the reply, "and therefore you will not wear silk stockings!" And so the matter ended.

But to return to the daily routine. Tea was at four o'clock and sometimes in the springtime Choura would be taken for a drive in the Island Park where it was as fashionable to drive at that hour, as it used to be in Hyde Park during the London season, until the advent of the motor-car which did not lend itself to such slow progress. Dinner was at six, and at seven Choura was always sent to bed, though on one night in the week she was allowed to stay up later in order to attend a dancing class. This class, held at the home of one of her aunt's friends, was a great joy to her, and she and twelve or so children of about the same age, learnt to waltz and to dance the Polonaise and Mazurka. Choura revelled in these occasions, partly because she loved dancing and partly because it brought her into association with other children.

Another break in the week's routine occurred on Wednesday afternoons, for Wednesday was Mme. Gotovzeva's reception day and her friends would often ask to see Choura, who, having been put into a nice clean dress, would be brought down by her governess and required to say "How do you do" to all the guests, who were certain to exclaim that she was just like a doll because she was so small, and would then proceed to ask her questions which appeared to her to be stupid but which she was obliged to answer politely, so altogether she was much relieved when the affair was over.

Of course she continued to see her sister, for Helen had by this time been adopted by a widow lady who also lived in St. Petersburg, so that the two children were never completely separated, though the elder girl was destined to have a much less crowded life than the younger, for she was married and settled in a home of her own shortly before her sister left on her eventful tour of Western Europe.

The only changes that disturbed this routine were a Christmas in Moscow at the house of an aunt of Mme. Gotovzeva, who was especially kind to Choura, letting her see her enormous store of jams of different kinds, and introducing her for the first time to rose petal jam, which the child enjoyed, finding the idea of eating rose petals very romantic. Among other recollections of Moscow were the skaters, gliding to music, and the largest Christmas tree that she had ever seen in her life! Altogether she enjoyed herself very much.

There was another happening which pleased her too, for on

attaining her fifth birthday, she found that in the future her
governess would take her to a Kindergarten every morning
instead of giving her lessons at home, and that was pleasant
because she was always happy in the company of others.

And so life progressed peacefully enough until that day when
she learnt of her aunt's decision to marry General Batianov,
which meant a new home for both of them and new relations
for Choura.

General Michael Ivanovich Batianov was one of the best-
known military figures in St. Petersburg, for he had actually
served under four Tsars, beginning his career at the age of sixteen under Tsar Nicholas I during the Turkish War and retiring
during the reign of Nicholas II, having in the interim held many
high positions, including that of Commander of the armies
of the Caucasus, and even after his retirement he was considered
one of the greatest military experts in Russia and frequently
wrote articles on army matters. He had already been twice
married and had nine children, though only those of his second
wife, two sons and a daughter, Maria, were living at home at
the time of his third marriage. General Batianov's second wife,
the mother of these three of his children, had been half English,
and had bequeathed to her daughter Maria a certain placidity
of character, in addition to the habit of eating toast and marmalade at breakfast, and little Choura, eating her toast, began to
consider herself half English also, a fact which she recalled with
pleasure when, many years later, she came to live and work in
London.

To one who had already nine children the addition of a tenth
did not seem to make much difference, and indeed the General
appears to have taken a fancy to Choura, and on one occasion
gave her five roubles, the first money she had ever possessed.
Thrilled to the core, she announced: "I shall buy a house."

"It is not enough to buy a house," said her aunt.

"Then I will buy you a dress," said Choura.

"Thank you very much, but I'm afraid that would cost too
much also. You had better buy something for yourself," was
the reply, and after much thought Choura decided, "I will buy
a house then for my dolls," and this, eventually, she did.

Choura thoroughly enjoyed all the excitement of the huge
Batianov house during, and for a week after, the wedding.
Then things began to calm down. The newly-married pair left

for Paris where they were to spend their honeymoon; the sons and daughters of the first wife, with their families, returned to their respective homes; and Choura went to spend her holidays with an aunt in the Crimea.   She enjoyed this journey very much, especially when, on nearing her destination, she passed through the mountains and saw field upon field of red and yellow poppies. which she thought beautiful.   But she got into grave trouble with this aunt for amusing herself by posing and dancing little steps before the mirror.   No one in St. Petersburg had ever interfered with this amusement or thought it harmful, but now she was accused of vanity, and punished by being sent to bed whenever she was found so employed.   But in spite of crying herself to sleep the lure of the dance was too strong, and Choura always returned to her mirror.

A year after her aunt's second marriage, Alexandra Danilova passed her seventh birthday and was sent to school in the following January.   At that time in Russia all little girls were sent at the age of seven to a day school, or "Gymnasia", where they remained for one or two years until old enough to enter an "Institute" where they lived until the age of eighteen, when they were introduced into society.   So Choura, like all the other children, left home at nine o'clock every morning, carrying her lunch in a little basket; she was accompanied by her governess, who escorted her to the school and fetched her home again at four in the afternoon.

In the meanwhile Mme. Batianova was trying to decide to which "Institute" she would send her, when fate intervened and Choura took her first step towards her future career.   Dancing lessons were included in the curriculum at the Gymnasia, and there she soon became noticeable for her unusual grace of movement, so much so that she won a prize for her dancing and was not unnaturally included among those children who were chosen to perform at the annual Christmas entertainment.

The sketch in which she made this, her first, appearance included a scene where a child chased a butterfly.   Choura was the butterfly, and the tiny figure in a yellow dress flitting hither and thither elicited great applause from the audience. She herself was much pleased with the dress which she was allowed to wear again at a children's masked ball in the holidays.

Some time after the Christmas concert she was found by her cousin Boris, who frequently came to the nursery to play with her, standing before the glass on the tips of her toes—*sur les pointes* in the language of ballet. Boris, surprised and impressed, told his step-mother what he had seen, with the result that the reluctant child was brought downstairs and requested to repeat the performance.

Uncertain as to whether or no she were doing something wrong, she complied, and her aunt, amazed, took this as definite proof that she had a talent for dancing, or, as Alexandra Danilova herself expresses it: "One day I just get on my toes and my aunt think I am second Pavlova and she decide to send me to Theatre School." Later on, when her aunt asked her if she would like to become a dancer, little Choura, who had never even seen a ballet, unhesitatingly answered, "Yes!" As soon as this plan for the child's future became known there was a storm of protest from the various relatives, their chief objection being that it was not customary for young girls of good family to enter the Theatre School. It was, of course, a very great break with tradition, and many of Mme. Batianova's friends would come to call and say "Please let us see your little Chourotchka—we hear that she is going to the Theatre School," almost as though she were a freak.

Mme. Batianova, convinced that her niece had genius, stood her ground and made application to the authorities for her admission to the Ballet School. Some difficulty was encountered because she was below the usual age for entry, but fate was on her side, and on successfully passing all the preliminary examinations, Alexandra Danilova, at the age of eight and a half years, became a pupil of the most famous dance school in the world, where she was to spend the next nine years of her life. Mme. Batianova never lived to see her prophecy fulfilled, for she died just one year later, but her niece always pays tribute to her foresight, saying: "I think my aunt was very clever woman to know I would be good dancer. The family was against it, but my aunt was very sure."

Chapter II

THE BALLET SCHOOL : I

THE IMPERIAL THEATRE SCHOOL in St. Petersburg, now called the Choreographic Technicum of Leningrad, was, during the Imperial *régime*, and still is, renowned throughout the world for being the greatest institution of its kind in existence, and, as the number of pupils received for training was strictly limited, admission was much sought after and difficult to obtain. As a preliminary measure all candidates were required to submit to an exhaustive medical examination, during which special attention was paid to the condition of the heart and lungs. Those who survived this test were sent before an Artistic Committee which was composed of the Directors and Teachers of the School and the *ballerine* of the Maryinsky Theatre. Here the children stood in line, each holding a little *carnet*, while the examiners walked up and down looking at them carefully, asking their names, and noting in each *carnet* the number of marks which they thought the child deserved. The whole object of the examination was to select those children who, besides being well-proportioned, naturally graceful, and pleasing to the eye, were possessed of personal charm or some other attribute likely to contribute to their success on the stage. Then followed the Educational Examination, when, after having satisfied the teachers that they could read, write, and answer a few simple questions, the survivors were accepted for admission to the Ballet School for one year on probation.

At the time that Alexandra Danilova's aunt applied for her niece's admission there were three hundred and fifty candidates present at the medical examination, and of these, only two hundred and eighteen were allowed to go before the Artistic Committee, where eighteen were chosen to enter the school, and so, at eight and a half years of age, being one year younger than her companions, Alexandra Danilova entered the Theatre School and was launched into the world of the dance to sink or swim as best she could.

During the first few years of their training the pupils could either live at home and attend the classes daily, or become

MARIA BATIANOVA

THAMAR KARSAVINA IN "LE PAVILLON D'ARMIDE"

internes, in which case the parents were required to pay for board and lodging. Mme. Batianova, wisely deciding that children were better with companions of their own age, sent her little niece straightway as a boarder, and once the initial strangeness had worn off the child was very happy.

Her first day she enjoyed, finding school very much like the "Gymnasia", though somewhat stricter. She was delighted with her long cornflower-blue dress, as an *interne*, with its white pelerine and two aprons, white for Sundays and black for the rest of the week, and was glad that she did not have to wear the brown dress which was the lot of the *externes*, and just like that which she had already worn at the "Gymnasia". But as evening approached she began to feel lonely and very homesick, for the huge dormitory where she was to sleep was not reassuring, and seemed quite unlike her little room at home. It contained forty-eight beds, each with a table beside it, and had an alcove with a further fifteen of each where the senior pupils slept. Each bed had a tablet above it inscribed with the name of the child to whom it belonged, but there was no other furniture as the children dressed and undressed in a special room where each had a cupboard for her clothes. When speaking of her first day in the school Alexandra Danilova always says: "It was all right until I go to bed, but then I weep and weep when the door shut out my home, but afterwards I adore the school."

On their first arrival each child was allotted to one of the five maids whose business it was to supervise the washing, and to comb their hair, only the senior class being exempt from this ministration, so that each maid was responsible for about eight or ten children at one time.

When the new pupils had been about two months in the school they were given each night after dinner an additional dancing class, where each little girl was taught by one of the senior pupils, who in some cases not only gave them a lesson, but tried to take care of them in other ways as well, coming to talk to them at bed-time and taking an interest in their personal welfare. Choura was extremely lucky in her pupil teacher, Maria Sherer (now better known as Mme. Bekefi), a beautiful and clever girl of Hungarian extraction, who was very popular in the school. Mme. Bekefi herself declares that Choura was one of the most charming children possible, and describes her as being "very thin, with long wavy hair and enormous eyes, looking just like a newly-hatched little bird gazing wide-eyed at the world about her." She was possessed of a hauntingly pathetic quality which made everyone want to protect and take care of her, though this was in fact very difficult of accomplishment owing to her independence of character.

Choura, however, became much attached to Maria, and wept bitterly when at the end of the year she finished her time of training in the schools and passed into the Imperial Ballet.

The strictness of the discipline imposed on the pupils was extreme, but very few seem to have resented it in any way. New pupils were given three days' grace in which to learn the rules, after which time punishments were awarded without any explanation, nor were excuses accepted by the authorities— a child must conform and obey or take the consequences. Punishments varied according to the gravity of the crime, minor offences being followed by deprivation of sweets after lunch, while the next degree of crime caused the offender to remain standing under the clock in the corridor, a position which ensured her being seen by all the pupils coming from the classes as well as by the boys on their way upstairs to their own department, and they of course would mock at the small sinner doing penance, while the older girls would remark: "Oh, it's Danilova to-day, is it?" and look reproachfully at her, all of which was most unpleasant.

"I stand there once," says Danilova, "but I never stand again." From which one gathers that the punishment, though disagreeable, was effective. However, the greatest and most dreaded penalty of all was that of being kept in school on Saturday evening, or in extreme cases all day Sunday, instead of being allowed to go home.

The school day started with a wash under the cold tap, summer or winter, followed at eight o'clock by a breakfast of tea and bread. At nine came lessons and at ten a dancing class which continued until twelve noon. A quarter of an hour later came lunch—meat, spaghetti, and vegetables—after which the pupils walked in the garden until one, when they went to various classes until five o'clock. An interval followed to allow them to wash their hands and tidy their hair before dinner at five-thirty, which consisted of soup, some other dish, and dessert. Then came another dancing lesson, that given by the senior pupils, followed by a light supper of *kasha*, a sort of porridge, and finally bed for all at nine. Each class lasted for forty-five minutes, with a short interval for rest before the next class began.

This seems a hard life for children of nine years old, yet the greatest care was taken of the pupils, and those who were considered too thin or who were delicate in any way were given extra nourishment—eggs in the morning, milk at lunch-time, and again milk and black bread in the afternoon. Little Choura, being small for her age and very thin, had all the extras, and oh, how she hated the milk! But in spite of all the extra diet she remained tiny throughout her school years. A curious habit obtained at breakfast, for butter, being only supplied to delicate children, was a luxury and much coveted, for which reason the owner of the butter would part with half her ration in exchange for some other delicacy at another meal. In Choura's case it was pastry at dinner. "I do not like to give up half my butter," she explains, "but when they tell me I will have two pastry twice a week then I do not mind, for I like very much the pastry!"

But apart from such bargaining she could be very generous with her butter, for she would often persuade Maria Sherer, whom she so much admired, to take the remaining half in token of affection, and how could anyone, faced with dry bread for breakfast, manage to refuse such an offer? It must be stated that Maria did not always deserve it, for when she had an interesting novel she would take it to the class-room where she was to give Choura a lesson, and, concealing it under her apron, would tell Choura to do a certain movement twenty times while she settled down to read in peace, until a little voice announced: "Please, I have finished." "Repeat with the other foot," was the reply, but, the book once finished, the lesson would progress normally. In contradiction to this parsimony in the matter of butter the authorities were generous with sugar, and every child took at least four lumps in each cup of tea, which, it may be added, Danilova still does!

The daily walks were not always taken in the garden, for at least once or twice a week the children went outside the school, one governess taking them always down a road behind the Bazaar, where there was no one to see them and nothing of any interest to be seen. The other, however, preferred to walk round the palace of the Dowager Empress, where the children could look into the courtyard and see the soldiers at the gates, and it was a joy to be able to stop for a second and gaze up into the face of a sentry under his huge helmet, always hoping one would not be noticed and reprimanded on the way home.

Friday of course was a red-letter day, for all, beginning with the youngest class, went to .the Russian steam baths. The *Bania*, or Bath House, being situated in one of the courtyards of the school, the children marched down there trying to undo as many of their clothes as possible on the way, for much glory was attached to the child who could be the first to enter naked into the bathroom, with the result that many small pairs of panties were incontinently shed upon the garden path. Once inside, the child would be thoroughly scrubbed by the maid who was responsible for her cleanliness, when she could remain in the hot room until she wished to take a shower, which could be either warm or cold according to her fancy. Of course the shower led to many practical jokes—"Let me get you a nice warm shower," being usually the prelude of a stream of unpleasantly cold water, while the shouts and screams would be such that the matron in charge would be obliged to intervene. But the greatest day of all at the *Bania* was the first day of term, for no child was ever allowed to go directly into the school— they went straight to the bath, this time without strewing clothes on the way, had their bath, and then recounted all their holiday adventures under the shower before dressing in the school uniform and going up to the class-rooms.

The education given in the Ballet School was almost identical with that of the Russian Institutes, with the addition of such special subjects as (in addition to dancing) French, Music (piano playing was compulsory), and Aesthetics, while after the Revolution the curriculum was still further enlarged to include English, German, Geometry, and histories of Art, Costume, and the Dance, which latter were so much appreciated that the children would even discuss them at supper. But Aesthetics which they disliked, "flew away because no one could ever understand what was being talked about!" All these lectures were given by professors from the University, so that it will be seen that the Ballet School was in no way behind the usual educational establishments throughout the country.

The dancing training proceeded at the same time as the general education, pupils being divided into Junior, Middle, and Senior divisions. For the dancing classes the pupils changed their long-skirted blue uniform for special dancing frocks of a

greyish colour, and if later they attained particular distinction
they were given a pink dress as a reward, while in the senior
division, only the most outstanding pupils were promoted to
white dresses, and there were rarely more than two or three of
these. Unfortunately, the administrators under the Soviet
suppressed the coloured dresses as being out of keeping with
Communist ideals.[1]

From the second year the children began to study character
dancing and ballroom dancing, while in the last two years they
were taught supported *adage* and mime with the boys of the
class corresponding to their own. Speech training was also
considered essential, and classes were held to teach the correct
use of make-up.

An examination in dancing (as well as in educational subjects)
was held at the end of each school year, and those who in their
first year of training failed to satisfy the examiners were forthwith dismissed from the school.

In addition to their training, the actual experience gained by
the pupils while still in the school was invaluable, for, from
the beginning of their second year onwards, the children appeared
in opera and ballet at the Maryinsky Theatre whenever their
presence was required, while the Theatre would make use of a
pupil from the Ballet School if there were a child's role in any
of their productions. After the Revolution the pupils also danced
in the opera ballets at the Mikhailovsky Theatre where light
operas were given and where they supplied all the elves and fairies
for *A Midsummer Night's Dream*. In this way they gained a
knowledge of the theatre in all its aspects such as no other ballet
school is able to provide for its pupils even at the present time.

One of the great advantages of employing pupils from time
to time in the theatre was that they were thus enabled to see
all the great dancers of the day, including those who would in
all probability have ceased to dance in public by the time the
children had passed out of the school. In this way, Choura,
who started to work on the stage during her second year of
training, was able to see such stars as Kshesinskaya, Preobrazhenskaya, Egorova, Pavlova, Vladimirov, and her special
favourite, Karsavina.

Both Kshesinskaya and Preobrazhenskaya had already

[1] When the writer visited the Choreographic Technicum in Leningrad
in 1937 all the Juniors were dressed in pink and the Seniors in white.

retired, but they returned to dance at special charity performances during the war; Kshesinskaya in *The Talisman*[1] (where she danced a *"Coda"* which was so popular that she would have to repeat it as many as seven or eight times), and Preobrazhenskaya in *Arlequinade*[2]. On one memorable occasion, they both danced in *La Fille du Pharaon*[3], as the Queen and Princess respectively, and had a wonderful mimed scene together which was something to be remembered, as both excelled in that difficult art.

Kshesinskaya impressed Choura by her wonderfully graceful manner of descending a staircase, for she frequently made her first appearance on a terrace or balcony and so was obliged to come downstairs to reach the level of the stage. She could also run on her toes with such speed and lightness that she seemed like a butterfly skimming backwards and forwards across the scene, though curiously enough her feet were not beautiful to look at. Her dancing was so vivid (*con brio* is the musical equivalent) that she was bound to make a very definite impression on her audience, and especially upon the children from the school.

Choura had ample opportunity to observe Kshesinskaya, for in one act of *The Talisman*, she and several other children sat on a raised platform, supposed to represent a cloud, from which they had an excellent view, while in another scene, eight children, of whom she was one, together with four *coryphées*, represented little fires circling round the stage during the *adage*.

Olga Preobrazhenskaya was also a very clever dancer, and one who had the distinction of being the last Russian *ballerina* to be wholly trained in the Italian style, all her successors being of the Russian school, which is a combination of the best points of both the Italian and French methods. Many years later Choura was again to meet Mme. Preobrazhenskaya who still directs one of the best ballet schools in Paris, where she has taught many of the young dancers of the present day.

Lubov Egorova, at that time one of the reigning *ballerine* of the Maryinsky Theatre, was especially noted for her very beautiful hands and for the manner in which she used them. Her chief roles were Odette in *Le Lac des Cygnes*, in which she gave the impression that her hands were wings, Aurora in *La*

---

[1] Ballet by Marius Petipa, first produced 1889.

[2] Ballet by Marius Petipa, first produced 1900.

[3] Ballet by Marius Petipa, first produced 1862.

Belle au Bois Dormant (*The Sleeping Princess*), and the leading part in *Evnika* (*Eunice*), the Greek ballet produced by Michel Fokine under the inspiration of Isadora Duncan, in which Vera Fokina, wife of the choreographer, danced the "*Dance of the Seven Veils*", where also, in order to conform to the rules of the theatre (which forbade bare-footed dancers) special tights had to be woven with glove fingers for each toe in order to give the illusion of bare legs and feet!

Fokine was one of the earliest people to single out Choura from her companions on the stage, for, when he produced Gluck's *Orphée* he made use of the children as Cupids, in which guise they shot real arrows from small bows, a procedure which required much rehearsal in order to avoid accidents, and which naturally enough they adored.   For some reason Fokine approved of Choura's efforts and called to his wife to come over and see her—"for this is a very capable girl, Vera," he said.   Choura specially liked Fokine's opera ballets, where the whole opera was danced, even the singers taking up plastic poses, which she describes as being "very beautiful".

Pierre Vladimirov, who was the leading male dancer at this time, was a remarkable man as well as a very handsome one. He was an excellent dancer who paid as much attention to the interpretation of a role as he did to the actual dancing of it, and even went so far as to have his costumes made specifically for him from the designs of his friend Gontcharov, who was also a member of the company, though for this he was somewhat criticised by the *balletomanes*. Possessed of great elevation, Vladimirov seldom or never walked off the stage, but would leap into the wings over the heads of the *corps de ballet* if they were sitting or kneeling on the stage, or over their shoulders if they were standing, in a fashion truly wonderful, and it is not surprising to know that he was the darling of the public as well as of the Ballet School.

One of his more spectacular feats was performed as a Wind, in *The Talisman*, when he "flew" from the level of the sixth floor on a wire to the ground, landing on one leg *en arabesque*— a very effective and dangerous feat! In this ballet he also danced to the music of a harp which hitherto was considered only suited to the dancing of a woman.   Choura was especially thrilled when she saw him with Karsavina during a rehearsal of *Les Préludes*, a ballet by Fokine to the music of Liszt.   It was more modern in style and choreography than anything which she had hitherto seen and she greatly admired it.

Tamara Karsavina was of course her ideal from the moment when she returned to Russia after a long season with Diaghilev, and the children saw her when she came to rehearse a minuet for a charity performance without changing into practice costume and drew all eyes to her lovely Parisian clothes! She was so lively, so intelligent, and so charming, that she conquered the hearts of the entire school, and when Choura met her again years later with the Diaghilev company she fell under her spell no less deeply than before.

Of Anna Pavlova, on the other hand, the child Choura knew very little, for she only saw her dance once in the ballet *Don Quichotte*, of which she retained no very definite impression. It must of course be remembered that while Pavlova was better known outside Russia than almost any other dancer, she was far less known at home where, in fact, she was regarded as one of the "foreign *ballerine*"; she had left her country so early and stayed away so long.

Lydia Kyasht, the friend of Karsavina, was another who behaved in much the same way, for she was well known in England, but scarcely at all in Russia, and now Alexandra Danilova completes the trio of expatriated dancers, for while her name is known in Leningrad and Moscow, and her artistic reputation stands high, very few people actually saw her as a fully fledged dancer. They remember her as a rising star, but her full brilliance has never been revealed to them.

For some reason or another, Choura never had another opportunity of seeing Pavlova dance until the year before her death, and then only in two performances, the first with her own company in Cannes, and the second at the Théâtre des Champs-Elysées in Paris, where she danced the title-role in *Giselle*. On the first occasion Danilova found the whole programme unpleasing with the exception of the beautifully danced "*Mort du Cygne*", but of *Giselle* she cherishes a much happier memory—that of Pavlova running in shimmering radiance across the stage, appearing and disappearing just as a pearl slips from a broken string, a gleam of milky irridescent splendour, vanishing almost as soon as the eye perceives it.

GEORGES BALANCHINE

Photo: Raoul Barba, Monte Carlo

ALEXANDRA DANILOVA AND LEON WOIZIKOWSKY
IN "LES MATELOTS"

Chapter III

THE BALLET SCHOOL: II

ALEXANDRA DANILOVA'S first year in the school was
happy and she took her studies lightly, so much so that
when the annual examination was held she nearly met with
disaster as did most of the other children in her class. For, of
the original eighteen pupils, only five were accepted for further
training; of the remainder, ten were dismissed, and three, of
whom Choura was one, were allowed to continue for another
year on probation, which of course entailed her joining the new
class which she was to enter at the beginning of the next school
year. However, this prospect does not appear to have unduly
depressed her at the time, and it would seem that her interest in
the dance was not as yet wholly awakened, for, as will be seen,
she was capable of making great progress once her attention was
concentrated on her work.

The holidays, however, were bound to occasion her some
sadness, for her aunt, Mme. Batianova, had died recently, and
so once again the child passed into the care of one who was
partly a stranger to her. Maria Batianova, who now undertook
her upbringing, had so far shown very little interest in Choura,
as being the niece of her step-mother, with whom she never
interfered, but to whom she was always polite and respectful.
Now that the child seemed to belong solely to her, she began
to pay much more attention to her well-being, and gradually
grew very fond of her, and was never so happy as when she
was with Choura, learning to sew and make dresses for her
dolls, picking up tennis balls, or gathering mushrooms in the
forest, for Maria was always gentle with her charge, never
losing her temper, and always explaining what was right and
wrong when she had been naughty.

Maria would have had a good influence on any child. She
was at that time about twenty-five years old, tall and very
pretty, with black wavy hair, blue eyes, and a fair skin, while
in character she was calm and quiet, a clever mathematician,
and a good rider, skater, cyclist, and tennis player. Her influence
over her father and all the family was very considerable. She

allowed Choura to choose new wallpaper and furniture for her bedroom in the apartment at St. Petersburg, and encouraged her to keep all her possessions, dolls and books, neatly arranged therein. It was Maria, too, who took Choura to hear the opera, *The Barber of Seville*, with Chaliapin in the leading role, an opera the child adored and which made her laugh. Unfortunately, Maria could not encourage her to take part in the sports which she herself loved, for riding, skating, cycling, and swimming were forbidden joys to all pupils in the ballet school, but there were plenty of other interests to be found.

These particular holidays were spent at Hungerbourg near Narva in Esthonia, in a house which belonged to Choura, but which she of course lost during the Revolution. It was a charming white wooden country house with large gardens, standing in the pine woods and facing the sea, and having its own private beach of the whitest sand imaginable—just the sort of place which would delight a child. Here she had plenty of little playfellows, who during these particular holidays got up an entertainment at which of course Choura had to dance, doing so very successfully, this time as a doll, a role which must have suited her very well.

The greatest event of all was a circus to which Maria took her, and of which she thought for weeks afterwards, but which had a disastrous effect on her arms and legs, for being utterly without fear she tried to copy every trick she had seen, and was covered with cuts and bruises as a result. Only the fact that she was forbidden to go in a swing prevented her from using that as a trapeze and breaking her neck into the bargain! Indeed, her complete fearlessness was something with which her guardians had to reckon, for it was always leading her into danger; for instance, her aunt took her one day to a Turkish bath, and when, near the end of the proceedings, Choura saw her swimming in the pool, she jumped gaily in and, not knowing how to swim, was pulled out half drowned. She never seemed to realise that she could not always do what she saw others doing.

Her favourite amusement in the huge thirteen-roomed apartment in St. Petersburg was not very safe either, for she and her friends used to play "Travellers"—a game in which the "Traveller" has to go all round the room without once stepping on the floor. Of course, the General's study was the favourite place for this occupation as it contained a good deal of furniture, including several large ottomans, which were a great help.

However, the best of holidays come to an end, and by September Choura was back in the School and starting on her second year of work, which was rather more interesting than the first, as it allowed more scope for individuality. But the unvarying routine went on with nothing except Christmas, for which the pupils returned home, and Lent, to break the monotony. Lent was something of an event, for the first and last of the six weeks were very strictly kept, the pupils ate no meat, and there were neither dancing nor any other lessons, only quiet amusements such as drawing and reading being permitted. The children attended church every day and went to confession and communion, they also begged each other's pardon for any annoyances which they had caused; and, because it was a sort of holiday, Lent was very popular.

Spring also brought another interest into the life of the School, since it was the custom for each junior pupil to select as her own particular goddess one of the seniors who was finishing that year, and to show her preference in a suitable manner. This took the form of wearing a bow of the favourite's chosen colour, or in springtime of bringing home a twig or small branch of a tree which could be placed in water so that the leaves might unfold more quickly in the warm room. This was a pretty idea, and it filled the window of the senior's room with green shoots of every kind. Choura's first idols had been Maria Sherer and Olga Spessivtzeva, both of whom left at the end of her first year in the school, but later she transferred all her admiration to the *ballerina* Karsavina and did not change again.

It was at this time that Choura first came into contact with Alexander Monakov, artistic director of the Maryinsky Theatre. At this time it was he who chose the children who were to dance in certain ballets, and to this end they were all assembled in the great hall of the school to await his selection. The very first he picked out was Choura, the smallest of them all, and, finding her to be intelligent, he thereafter used her in all the ballets which required child dancers. He himself used to rehearse the children, and so well did he teach them that, when they attended the full rehearsals on Thursday, and the orchestra rehearsals on Friday, they never got out of place and knew exactly where they should pass between the other dancers. This was always a difficult feat, especially for Choura, who according to size led the others both on to and off the stage. Monakov, a very handsome man, was a brilliant character dancer, unequalled in Spanish, Polish, and Hungarian dances, and an excellent mime. As a teacher he was possessed of unlimited patience, never losing his temper with anyone who was slow at understanding or in learning a role.

And now Choura was approaching one of the turning points of her career, for the yearly examinations were drawing near and, if she failed again, it was not likely that she would be allowed a third year on probation.

For days before this event the pupils made expeditions to the little wooden church built by Peter the Great, there to pray for help, and to burn candles before the altar for a successful result. The dreaded day arrived, and to the amazement of everyone Choura passed at the top of her class, obtaining the highest number of possible marks, an achievement which entitled her to free board, lodging, and training for the rest of her time in the school. When asked, many years later, whether she had not had to work very hard in order to pass so well, she laughed and answered: "Oh, no! You see, I begin to get interested, and so I just work a little bit."

One of her school companions of that time, Vera Timé, relates how after Danilova's astonishing success in the examination, the authorities expected great things of her, and were not so severe with her for her numerous mischievous pranks as they would have been with anyone less talented. It is this same friend who gives a verbal picture of her as she was at the beginning of her third year at school "She was very small for her age, in fact quite tiny, and with her long wavy hair, little straight nose, pursed-up mouth, pointed chin, and round cheeks, looked just like a doll, while her eyes, which always seemed too large for her face, added to the illusion."

"She was very gay, sparkling, and mischievous, though occasionally she would spend a day wandering about unsmiling, with huge tragic eyes gazing drearily at the world about her. No one ever succeeded in discovering the reason for this unhappy mood, which would vanish as suddenly as it came, and which only served to increase the charm and mystery of little Choura."

Among the boy pupils, however, Choura had a quite different reputation. They admired her immensely, especially her long

ALEXANDRA DANILOVA IN "LE CARNAVAL"

ALEXANDRA DANILOVA IN "LES SYLPHIDES"

waving hair, and would write little notes to her as they did to all who took their fancy; but Choura, always reserved and aloof, never answered the letters or took any special notice of the writers, so that until the very end of her school days she retained their nickname for her—"the Grand Duchess."

It was about this time that Choura began to be recognised by the audience, for she was the pupil most frequently seen on the stage. Luckily for her, she was not subject to stage-fright, although on one occasion she suffered agonies before the performance for fear that her relatives would applaud in order to encourage her in her work. Applause from relatives was definitely forbidden in the Maryinsky, and her uncle and aunt knew that as well as she did, but this did not calm the child's fears since she was to appear alone for the first time. The ballet was *Le Pavillon d'Armide*, and in the last act two children, a boy and a girl, wander into the ruined pavilion, and, seeing the hero, who has dreamed the ballet, lying there fast asleep, they become frightened and run away. It was a very small part, but to Choura it was at least as great as the *ballerina's variation*, and she was terrified of her family's reaction! "Please, please, don't applaud!" she begged, and was much relieved when they promised to abide by the rules. Afterwards, her uncle asked her, "Where were you?" for he had not noticed her.

"I was there, indeed I was there," said Choura. "Why didn't you see me?"

And she was most indignant about it. Later she had a speaking part in the opera *Roussalka*, where she attracted the attention of Chaliapin, who asked her name and then picked her up and kissed her. Choura was much impressed, and later that night got into trouble in the school for refusing to wash her forehead before going to bed, saying that it was there that the great Chaliapin had kissed her!

Certainly it was her smallness that first attracted the public, and they became quite used to seeing her in front of all the other children; but she herself wished desperately to grow, for the others teased her so much about her size and doll-like appearance. However, she did not grow much taller for many years to come.

It was in the last act of *La Fille Mal Gardée*[1] that she had her first taste of fame, for there was a peasant dance, "*Sabotière*,"

[1] Ballet by Dauberval, first produced 1786.

C

for two children, a girl and a boy, danced in sabots, which always brought the house down. The girl was Evgenia Svekis and the "boy" Alexandra Danilova, and there was no evening when they danced that they did not have to give an encore before the public would allow the performance to proceed.

At the end of this, her third year in the school, Choura was moved out of the Junior Division where she had been taught first by Voronzov, and later by Mme. Varvara Rickliakova, into the Middle Division under Mme. Vera Zhukova; while in this class she was honoured by being chosen to dance at the pupils' annual performance. This performance was actually given to display the attainments of the Senior Class, the members of which were leaving the school that year, but in addition the most promising pupil from each division was given a small *variation*, and Choura once again became a "Butterfly," this time to the music of one of Chopin's *Etudes*. She danced well and quite enjoyed the whole affair, not feeling nearly as nervous as did her senior, to whom the performance was a grim trial of their skill.

The school year was divided into four "quarters", and at the end of each quarter the girls were assembled in the large hall of the school to await the arrival of *Mme. la Directrice* Varvara Ivanovna Lihocherstova, a beautiful woman with blue eyes and wonderful white hair, who had been trained at the famous Smolny "Institute", and of whom all the children stood greatly in awe. Having just handed to each pupil an envelope containing a list of her marks for the quarter to be taken home and given to her parents, Mme. Lihocherstova proceeded to read these aloud, and then continued with a list of awards and class promotions, and what was Choura's surprise one day when she was still in the Middle Division to hear herself awarded the coveted "pink dress" for her dancing. But if she were surprised, the rest of the school was more so, for never in its whole history had anyone outside the Senior Division received a "pink dress", and so there was much discussion, and envy in all directions.

The marks for the dancing examination fell into three categories—talent, work, and actual dancing. The maximum number of marks obtainable was twelve for Seniors, nine for the Juniors. The results would read something like this:

Talent	4		Talent	2
Work	3		Work	4
Dancing	4	or	Dancing	3
	—			—
Total	11		Total	9

It is interesting to note that those who shone during their first year were seldom brilliantly successful later, since the more artistically minded pupils did not find the one-two, one-two-three of the exercises at the bar very inspiring, and so their talent only appeared as their individuality was allowed to develop.

And so life went on, from school to holidays and then back again to school, but Choura's orbit was gradually widening, for Maria took her out with her on such Sundays as she was not dancing, and actually took her to the Maryinsky Theatre to see the ballet *Esmeralda*[1] (the first time that Choura had seen a ballet from the auditorium) and also to concerts and other entertainments, while, in addition, she improved the child's taste by discussing her likes and dislikes and by showing her why one style was better than another.

Presently, the first World War overshadowed Russia, though it actually brought very little change to the school, except rather shorter holidays, and, for Choura, the first of two narrow escapes from death. One day, when she was at home, her uncle showed her a German rifle which he had brought back from the front. Now Choura did not like firearms and said so, but her uncle laughed, picked up the rifle, and, pointing it at her, pulled the trigger. Choura, terrified, screamed and jumped to one side just in time, for the weapon, which her uncle had believed to be empty, was loaded, and the bullet whizzed past her ear.

General Batianov died during the latter half of the war just before the Revolution broke out, which was a merciful dispensation of Providence, for he was too old to have been able to adapt himself to the changing conditions in his native country. He was given a most imposing military funeral, and Choura in particular was much impressed by the enormous wreath of roses sent by the Tsar and thought it must be wonderful to be able to get such lovely red roses in February.

Then followed the Revolution which, however, did not

[1] Ballet by Jules Perrot, first produced 1844.

immediately change the routine of the Ballet School, although those children who lived at home would tell curious stories of how one or other of their relatives had disappeared, and no one knew what had become of them. Here, Choura had a second escape from death, which took place in the school itself. The pupils were forbidden to look out of the windows during the Revolution, but one day, hearing shots in the street, the temptation to see what was going on was irresistible, and the whole class packed itself in the window. They did not see much, however, for an observant soldier saw them and fired straight at the window, missing Choura's head by a few inches, scattering broken glass everywhere, and causing the whole class to fall in a heap on the floor. They did not attempt to look out of the window again!

Some months later food began to get scarce in St. Petersburg, and there were rumours that the Germans were invading Russia and getting near the city, so Maria decided to leave home for a while and go to the district of the Kuban Cossacks where food was more easily obtainable, and where her invalid brother and Choura would be in less danger. They all left by train without any particular difficulty, taking with them a cook and two maids, and settled in an apartment in the little town of Yeask, where they lived quietly and peacefully, for a whole year. But they all found it very dull, especially Choura, who had to practise her dancing every day by herself and have all her other lessons given her by Maria.

After the year had passed they decided to return to St. Petersburg, for the German menace no longer existed and Maria wanted Choura to continue her education as before. To this end the maids were dispatched to prepare the apartment, while Maria, her brother, and Choura followed two days later, but they found that during their absence conditions had completely changed and it took them two weeks to reach the capital. The next surprise was furnished by the porter who dealt with their luggage, who, when offered money, refused it, saying: "You come from the country. Have you no bread?" Maria immediately offered him a loaf at which he gazed in amazement, saying, "I've not seen so much bread for weeks," and considered himself well paid.

When they arrived at their apartment they found that all the maids had disappeared taking with them many valuable

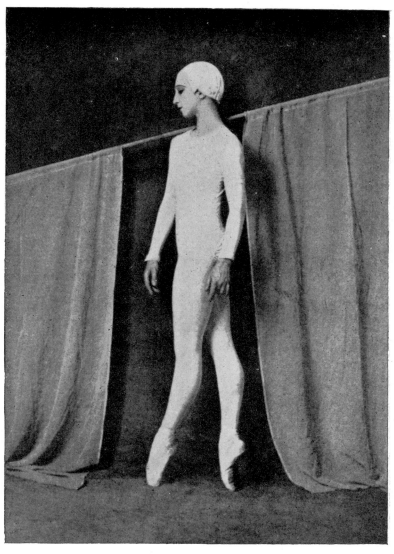

ALEXANDRA DANILOVA IN "ODE"

ALEXANDRA DANILOVA IN "LES FEMMES DE BONNE HUMEUR"

things, and Maria and Choura were left to do all the work. Shortly afterwards, they went to dine with one of Choura's uncles, who offered them a very poor dinner. Choura did not understand the reason for this, and, when offered potatoes, replied, "No, thank you. I don't eat potatoes." "Oh," said her uncle, "in three weeks, my dear, you will be glad to eat potato skins only."

"And," admits Choura sadly, "it was true."

When she returned to the school she found things were in many ways different, food was very scarce and became more so as time went on, until dinner consisted of "dirty water" soup and two spoonsful of *kasha*. Sugar declined to one lump, then to saccharine, and finally there was not even any of that left. Lunch consisted of potatoes and *kasha*, and then of one spoonful of *kasha* only; while supper was composed of first two tablespoons of *kasha* and then only one. Bread was reduced to one-eighth of a pound per person per day, an amount of which the hungry children made one mouthful, while, to make matters worse, they would talk to each other about the things which they would like to eat, and this made them feel really ill.

The cold also was terrible, and to combat it as many classes as possible were held in one room, the pupils wearing fur coats and overshoes, but even so their hands were frozen and writing was very difficult. The boy pupils, who lived in a separate division of the school, used to go into the garrets under the roof searching for wood left there for repairing the rafters, and this they would bring downstairs to be cut up and burned in the stoves, hence the little girls did all they could to be nice to the little boys so that their own classrooms might be warmed.

It was not only the school which was cold. The Maryinsky Theatre was unheated, and had to be closed for some months, but not before the *ballerine* had taken to dancing in woollen tights and with sweaters over their ballet dresses in an effort to keep warm. It is no wonder, therefore, that the children welcomed rehearsals in the afternoons, as it was easier to keep warm dancing than when sitting in a class-room.

Eventually the pupils were sent to sleep at home and came daily to the school, but food became scarcer and scarcer. The shops were empty of all eatables, the staple articles of diet being little cakes made out of coffee grounds, and potato or apple peelings. This state of things continued until the American

Red Cross took the school under its wing and provided food and firing for the children so that they could sleep and eat there once more.

But there was a lighter side, even to the Revolution. Late one evening there was a loud knocking at the door of the school and one of the mistresses went to open it. Outside she found some soldiers, the leader of whom stalked into the hall. "I have come to search for counter-revolutionaries," he announced. "We don't know how many may not be hiding here." The mistress led him through the class-rooms which were empty of all save the pupils. Then he said: "Where do you all sleep? I must search the bedrooms; someone might be hiding under the beds." So he was conducted to the dormitory, and the door opened upon that vast room with its sixty-three beds. The soldier stood appalled, and one girl, bolder than the rest, cried: "Please look under my bed!" "And mine!"

"And mine!" besought the others, but, without another look, the soldier turned and ran down the stairs and back to his comrades, hearing bursts of childish merriment on the stairway behind him!

The Bolsheviks, however, did try to be kind to the pupils, for, realising what deprivations they were undergoing, the authorities decided to give a Christmas party, a thing which had never happened before, as the children always went home for Christmas and of course had their own parties there. Now no one had a party and so there was one in the school, and even a Christmas tree, from which each child received a sweet cake and two nuts, while the presents which were given were chosen from one of the largest shops in Petrograd by a committee of the children themselves, and Choura much enjoyed that shopping. The thing which made the greatest impression on her, however, was the hitherto unknown fact of three boys arriving in blue serge suits instead of their school uniforms, and she thought they looked wonderfully handsome in their new clothes.

The Revolution taught Choura to realise that nothing in this world is secure. It is true that death had many times disturbed her life, but of financial difficulties she had had no experience, and how should she? As the child of rich parents and the niece of a family even more wealthy, she had taken material comfort for granted, and had even wondered a little why her companions should be surprised at her being brought to and from the school by a maid in a carriage with a pair of horses! Now she went home to an almost empty apartment. Her uncle was dead, the servants had run away, and Maria had moved with her invalid brother from their large thirteen-roomed apartment to a smaller one of five rooms only.[1]

Maria herself started to look for a job, which was difficult for her as she was considered too "aristocratic". In the end, however, being a good mathematician, she did manage to secure a post as cashier in a restaurant for sick people, from whence she was allowed to take home food for herself, and there she worked for two years. Choura did not like to think of her being reduced to such straits, and longed for the day when she could leave the school and support her, for all artists had a special allowance of food allotted to them by the Government. Maria was a very remarkable woman, for when, in the early days of the disturbance, she was told that an opportunity would be given her to go abroad, she refused even to contemplate the idea. Choura would have liked to go and could not understand why the offer was not accepted, but Maria told her that she did not approve of *emigrés*, and that, as she had lived in her own country during its good days, so she would remain there during its bad; she felt it her duty to do so, and from that decision no one could move her.

Choura was now seeing life in the raw and learning that even with money it was almost impossible at that time to obtain what one needed, for money now had absolutely no value, and when she and her aunt tried to obtain food in the market they had to take curtains from the apartment, or chairs, and exchange them with the peasants for food. The peasants were not anxious for money, for at that time they had enough food for themselves and their families, but they were not above bartering food for some article which took their fancy, and in this way people managed to obtain just enough to keep themselves alive.

In the school also Choura found herself growing up and becoming, in company with the other seniors, a passionate guardian of ballet tradition, for living as they did in a rapidly

[1] Servants' quarters and kitchen were not included in the number of rooms mentioned in an "apartment" in Russia, so that "five rooms" meant two maids' rooms and all servants' quarters in addition to the five rooms for the family.

changing world, these girls felt, not unnaturally, that without their precept and example all the old customs of the school would shortly disappear. Many of the pupils had been taken away by their relatives (either abroad or to parts of Russia where food was more plentiful), so that those who remained needed to be doubly strict in their training of the younger ones. This, however, did not prevent Choura, as a Senior, from having a large number of admirers among the Juniors, who wore a bow of her favourite shade of blue and who expected her in the evening to sit on each of their beds in turn to talk to them and kiss them "Good night ".

But even so she still remained a terrible tease, her chief method of annoying others at this time being to retire into a corner and indulge in a whispered conversation with a friend (one Choura Barash), taking great care that though all the others could see them, they could not hear what was said, and when at length curiosity became so great as to cause an interruption, they would say: "Go away, you are not old enough to understand; we are talking secrets." And even though they could not possibly have had an important secret, yet the two Chouras always succeeded in rousing the others to fury, which was exactly what they meant to do !

The last year in school was very important, and the pupils counted the days from three hundred and sixty-five downwards until the great day when they would be free, calling out the exact number each morning as soon as they woke up, but, alas for Choura, three hundred and sixty-five days for her classmates meant double that number for her, since, at the end of her training period, she was still considered too young to leave the school in spite of having passed two years in the most junior class, and so she did *two* "last years", passing through the hands of innumerable teachers during her time in the Senior Division, owing to the death of the first of these, Mme. Clavdia Koulichevskaya, who was succeeded for a short time by Mme. Julie Sedova (who now teaches in Nice and Cannes and has often taught the "Ballet Russe" in Monte Carlo). She in turn gave place to Mme. Elizaveta Gerdt (then a *ballerina* at the Maryinsky), to Victor Semenov, and finally to Mme. Agrippina Vaganova, who to-day still holds the same position.

But at last the extra year was over, the examinations were past, and the annual performance about to be given. That year, for some unknown reason, it took place in the Maryinsky itself, instead of, as usual, in the school theatre; moreover, owing to some complications in the school, it was decided upon only at the last minute, when the dances were hurriedly arranged by Mme. Preobrazhenskaya who was then teaching one of the junior classes. For Choura she chose a *pas de deux* from Delibes' ballet *Sylvia*, with Nicholas Efimov as her partner, but although they were both considered to have danced well, the *variation* itself was uninteresting. At this time Danilova learned that she and her great friend, Lydia Ivanova, were considered the most promising pupils in the school.

Then last of all came the farewell evening. The seniors passing out had cried "Only one more day" when starting work that morning, and now they were standing before the director of the theatre in the Great Hall, all eyes centred upon them. Five young girls in white dresses (made from material purchased with a permit from the Government) were all who remained of the original eighteen who had entered the school. They were presented with bouquets of flowers and should have been given volumes of the Russian classics as souvenirs of their school days, but, since the classics were no longer obtainable, there were no books.

Then the director made a speech to the small group of girls in which he referred to their achievements and congratulated them on their work, speaking as though they were already dancers rather than pupils; continuing, he told them what would be expected of them in the future, and concluded by wishing them a happy holiday before telling them to report on the following September 1st at the Maryinsky Theatre, or, as it was then called, the "Government Academic Theatre of Opera and Ballet."

Choura's years of preparation for her chosen career were over, and now she was no longer little Choura Danilova, the pupil, but Mlle. Alexandra Danilova, a fully-fledged member of the Russian State Ballet Company.

Chapter IV

THE MARYINSKY THEATRE

BEFORE the Revolution, three of the best-known theatres in
Petrograd were under the management of the Imperial
Government, and when the Soviet came to power they continued to direct this group under the title of the "State Theatres."
The three concerned were the Maryinsky Theatre, or Government Theatre of Opera and Ballet, where Grand Opera and
Ballet were given; the Mikhailovsky for Light Opera; and the
Alexandrinsky for Drama. There was one director in charge of
the whole group, but each theatre had, in addition, its own
director and staff. The Maryinsky Theatre had a director, an
artistic director for Opera, and another for Ballet, and a *régisseur*
who had complete charge of the actual performance, with four
assistant *régisseurs*. A matron took charge of the young girls
of the *corps de ballet*, being responsible for their punctuality on
the stage, for their replacement by an understudy if they were
ill, and, most difficult of all, for seeing that they did not make
too much noise in the huge dressing-room which was "like a
horse-box".

The casting of the ballets was done by the artistic director
who attended all the major rehearsals, but it was the *régisseur's*
business to see that each artist knew what role he or she was to
dance and when they should attend rehearsal. The life of the
theatre was strenuous; class from half-past ten until twelve
noon, attended by all except, perhaps, the *ballerine* (who could
take their lessons in private), then a half-hour rest interval,
during which the dancers ate the sandwiches which they had
brought with them and drank tea which was provided on the
premises. At half-past twelve rehearsal started and continued
until four o'clock, though it could, if necessary, be prolonged
a little longer. Tea and sandwiches were available all the time
for those who wished to buy them. The performances, whether
of opera or ballet, started at seven-thirty, and sometimes, after
the Revolution, the dancers who only appeared in the first or
third act of an opera, would rush out to dance at some club where
an entertainment was being given, and then come back again to

42

the theatre. It was a hard life, complicated, for Danilova, by the fact that she was obliged to walk to and from the theatre, which took her forty minutes each way, as there were no cabs or other conveyances to be had at that time in Petrograd.

Rehearsals were held in the rehearsal room which was in a special wing of the Ballet School building. It took up two stories of the building and the whole width, having windows on both sides, a gallery which ran round the top, and its floor sloping down towards a row of mirrors at one end. The room was quite familiar to all the school pupils for they had rehearsed there, but when on the eventful September 1st the five young girls entered it for the first time as artistes of the theatre, its aspect was at once familiar and strange, for instead of the pupils, strictly disciplined, and wearing their school white, pink, and grey dresses, the room was alive with pretty girls in gay practice *tutus* of every colour of the rainbow, flitting hither and thither, laughing and chatting to one another like a cloud of butterflies. For the newcomers, that morning was something of an ordeal, for they saw all the admired and adored dancers of the company, from the *ballerine* downwards, and to each the young girls must say "Good morning", according to the strict etiquette of the Maryinsky Theatre, and to thus approach a *ballerina*, who had hitherto been a goddess who smiled at one from a distance, took a great deal of courage.

The morning classes for the company were given by Mme. Vaganova who also taught the Senior Class in the school, but on that first morning Danilova was the only one of the five novices who had sufficient strength of mind to attend, and she, quite overcome by the presence of such distinguished dancers, hid herself in a far corner and worked very hard. However, being the most junior member of the company present, she was called forth from time to time to sprinkle the floor with water, find the rosin for the seniors, or do any other odd job which might present itself! Nothing daunted, she attended class daily, worked most energetically, and at the end of the season was rewarded by the directors for her diligence. She was chosen as having worked harder and made more progress than anyone else in the company, and given a special prize intended for such work as hers, but seldom either earned or awarded. It was the privilege of the winner to choose his or her own reward, but when Danilova appeared before the directors and they asked her what she would prefer, she amazed them all by asking for "four *sagen* (a large measure) of firewood, for it is so very cold at home". Though surprised, they proved not unsympathetic, and she received the fuel, which was badly needed.

When the first rehearsal started, Alexandra Danilova found that she had been placed with the cream of the *corps de ballet*, those who danced in *Chopiniana* (the original version of *Les Sylphides*) or as the friends of the hapless heroine in *Giselle*. It was no mean honour for a pupil straight from school to pass directly into the front rank of a *corps de ballet* of two hundred and fifty dancers, and it seemed a good omen for her stage career.

Rehearsals were conducted by Fedor Lopokov (brother of Lydia Lopokova) the artistic director at that time. Lopokov, a tall thin man, with blue eyes and fair hair, which he wore very long according to the mode of that day in Petrograd, was much liked and respected by all the young artists, for he took great pains with them, helping them to understand their roles both in the artistic and interpretive sense and encouraging them to ask questions on any subject connected with their work. He was the first person to suggest to the dancers that they should study music other than that specially written for ballet, and that they should attend lectures on Art in its various forms as well as visit museums and galleries. He insisted that all details in his own ballets should be historically and artistically correct, and made the young dancers feel that they were really creating something of artistic worth rather than simply dancing a role.

Danilova, who was at first much in awe of him, began later to realise that he was interested in her work, and so found herself gradually becoming a member of his chosen group of young dancers. He always called her "Coucoushka (Little Cuckoo), perhaps because she still gazed wide-eyed at the world, and advised her to attend a series of symphony concerts then being given, saying that knowledge of such music would be useful to her later on.

Lopokov was very strict at rehearsal, and there is a story of a dancer who came to rehearsal in her ordinary clothes and worked with the others who were all in practice dress. Lopokov looked at her but said nothing, until the others lay on the floor while she remained standing, when he said: "Why don't you lie down?" She, smiling, replied: "But I'm not dressed.

ALEXANDRA DANILOVA BEFORE A PERFORMANCE

ALEXANDRA DANILOVA IN "LES DIEUX MENDIANTS"

I'm going to a party." "It's not my fault," said Lopokov, "that you are not properly dressed, but at rehearsals you will do as the others do. Please lie down." The girl lay down and finished the rehearsal properly, but by the end of the afternoon her dress was ruined.

It was during her second season at the Maryinsky, that Lopokov one day asked Danilova if she would be willing to work with him in her spare time on an experiment which he was anxious to make, and which might, or might not, prove to be of interest later on. She gladly agreed, and thenceforth worked with her friend Lydia Ivanova, Andrey Lopokov, brother of Fedor, and several other dancers on the "experiment", which proved to be a ballet to the music of Beethoven's *Fourth Symphony*, the subject of which was the Creation of the World. Produced later at the Marinsky it had a very mixed reception, half of the audience applauding loudly while the remainder shrieked and hissed, one Chinese gentleman in particular becoming almost serpentine in his efforts to express his disapproval! Danilova herself and Lydia Ivanova danced the principal roles in the second movement, where there was an *adage* for the two of them with all the male dancers in the ballet.

Lopokov's choreography was distinctly modern and it was in this ballet that Danilova met with syncopation for the first time in her life, being required to move her feet in one-two, one-two time, and her hands and arms in one-two-three, which she found very difficult at first, but she much enjoyed working for Lopokov, and always felt grateful to him for the help which he gave her at the very outset of her career.

Danilova was awarded her first "solo" at the final ballet performance of her first season, and the role chosen for her by the director was that of "*Prayer*" in Act 3 of Delibes' ballet *Coppélia*. But, as the dancer was required to wear her hair hanging loose on her shoulders, Danilova always declares that she was chosen for the suitability of her long waving hair rather than for the excellence of her dancing!

Then came the holidays, and incidentally a very pleasant surprise for her, when Serge Ponomarev, the chief *régisseur*, who was organising a group of twenty-five or thirty dancers to perform in clubs and garden theatres during the summer, asked her if she would care to be included among them. It was a great honour for a dancer in her first season and she was overjoyed, especially as she knew that many far more experienced dancers would have given their eyes to go but were not asked. The work was very hard, but the experience excellent, and there was always the chance that one of the leading dancers might fall ill, and then a junior would have to take her place and dance an important role, added to which the extra payment, sometimes in money, sometimes in bread, butter, or other provisions, was very welcome, for at that time everyone was poor, and food, firewood, and clothing were very difficult to obtain. Danilova herself had very few clothes, one navy blue dress, one costume, and one evening dress, while her shoes were almost worn out and shabby, and there was no immediate hope of being able to replace them. The only good things which could be bought were hats, and these were very smart, but not of much use when one needed shoes! She was fortunate in having several foreign acquaintances who, from time to time, brought her such small gifts as a pair of stockings, or gloves, or a little bottle of perfume from abroad.

Alexandra Danilova's second season at the Marinsky was a heavy one, for in addition to dancing in both Opera and Ballet, and the extra work she did with Lopokov, she was also working with a talented young choreographer, Georges Balanchivadze, who had been a fellow pupil of hers in the school. Balanchivadze, who was both musician and dancer, had very early in his training shown signs of possessing considerable choreographic talent, and had been asked to arrange dances for the school performances while still a pupil. Now, in addition to dancing at the Maryinsky, he was studying music at the Conservatoire and arranging concert performances in his spare time.

Owing to the lack of money and the difficulty of getting about, most people were compelled to spend their holidays at home, and this gave rise to all sorts of performances in public gardens, clubs, and elsewhere. Whenever possible Danilova danced with this group, which was composed entirely of young dancers, all of whom found his extremely modern, almost acrobatic, choreography very interesting.

There was one particularly lovely ballet which he arranged to Chopin's well-known *Marche Funèbre*, in which the dancers wore short black and grey tunics and knickers, and were bare-legged instead of wearing the usual tights. Balanchivadze was at that time a great admirer of Chopin, even going to the extent of wearing his hair long and drooping, and dressing himself in a black shirt and suit in imitation of his idol.

Occasionally he would dance in one of his own productions, but though he was really a classical and *demi-caractère* dancer, his greatest performance was always in the "*Lesghinka*", or dance with knives, of his native Caucasus, which is both wild and beautiful.

The authorities at the Maryinsky Theatre, however, did not approve of Balanchivadze's innovations and some time later a notice appeared on the Theatre call board, stating in no uncertain terms that any member of the State Ballet who continued to dance for him would forthwith be dismissed from the company, and so the "Evenings of the Young Ballet" came to an untimely end.[1]

It was at the beginning of this season that Danilova became obsessed with the desire to go abroad and complete her education in other lands. She had then no idea of joining the famous company of Diaghilev of whom she knew very little, except the episode of a certain well-known *ballerina*, who, after an enormously successful season with his company, was, on her return to Russia, sent to class for three months before she was considered good enough to reappear at the Maryinsky! But, apart from the desire to travel, which seemed impossible of realisation, she was at this time working more seriously than ever under the supervision of Elizaveta Gerdt. The three *ballerine* of the Maryinsky at this time were Elizaveta Gerdt, Olga Spessivtzeva, and Helen Loukom, each one very different from the other. Gerdt was possessed of a technique so perfect that it seemed impossible that any movement which she made could ever be bettered. Emotionally she was cold, but this was atoned for by the exquisite flawlessness of her dancing. Spessivtzeva also possessed a beautiful technique and was famed for her dramatic interpretations of classical roles, while Loukom, less strong technically, was a charming little person, all grace and emotion.

Mme. Gerdt is very proud to-day of the achievements of Alexandra Danilova, to whom she alludes as "my pupil", and to whom she gave much good advice, insisting that she pay particular attention to her hands and knees, for at that time she had just started to grow, and Gerdt affectionately called her

[1] Georges Balanchine.

"The Puppy", saying that she was all arms and legs. This has
not gone unrewarded, for the "Puppy" has the straightest knees
and most expressive hands of any dancer of the present day.
In addition, Alexandra Danilova was following Lopokov's
instructions and doing all she could to educate herself artistically, to which end she spent her free evenings in the box reserved
for the artistes in each of the State Theatres. Later, as her circle
of acquaintances widened, she used to get her friends to take her to
the other theatres, and in this way saw the famous Jewish Habima
Theatre, and the well-known actor, Alexander Moissi, in *Hamlet*,
besides many strange and interesting productions by Meyerhold
at the Alexandrinsky, where the whole tradition of the theatre
was turned upside-down by extreme modernism, much in the
same way as she and her fellow dancers were dancing in the old
classical ballets of Petipa and other masters at the same time as
in the modern works of Balanchivadze. But the dancer who
at this time made the greatest impression on her was Isadora
Duncan, who in 1924 paid a visit to Soviet Russia, and so impressed Alexandra Danilova that she declares that never since
then has she seen any artist of the modern school who is in any
way fit to be compared with her, and this in the days when she
was neither as young nor as beautiful as she had once been.

Suddenly and quite unexpectedly Danilova received her first
leading role. It was towards the end of her second season at
the Maryinsky that Lopokov produced, after Fokine, Stravinsky's ballet *L'Oiseau de Feu*, but with his own, rather modern,
choreography. Loukom was the *ballerina* chosen for the part
of the Firebird, but Lopokov insisted that Danilova should
learn it also, and he carried his point even though it nearly caused
a revolution in the company, and she danced it two or three
times, to the annoyance of all the *ballerine*.

Igor Schvezov, dancer, choreographer, and author of the
prizewinning autobiography, *Borzoï (Russian Somersault)*, was
in Russia at this time and saw Danilova's performances of this
role. He was kind enough to give the following particulars,
which are extremely valuable, since it is difficult to find anyone
outside Russia who was acquainted with her dancing at this
time.

"At her first performance Danilova amazed everyone by the
brilliance of her dancing in the first scene. She seemed to put
every ounce of energy and artistry which she possessed into her

ALEXANDRA DANILOVA IN "L'OISEAU DE FEU"

ALEXANDRA DANILOVA IN "LE BAL," 1928

work and the audience anxiously awaited her re-appearance.
Unfortunately, Danilova, in common with all very young
dancers when first they dance a leading role, had forgotten that
it was necessary to conserve a certain amount of strength for
the later scenes, and, having opened too brilliantly, found herself
utterly exhausted, indeed almost fainting on the stage, before
the conclusion of the ballet.

"At subsequent performances she succeeded in regulating
her energy better, so that without perhaps opening so brilliantly,
she danced in such a way as fully to justify Lopokov's choice
of her for the part."

Her partner was Boris Shavrov, and with him she fell ro-
mantically in love, for he would talk to her on the stage and kiss
her hand at the end of the performance, but when the curtain
fell the dream came to an abrupt end. Next day he would fail
to recognise her, because, while he was a leading dancer, she
was officially only a member of the *corps de ballet*, and, curiously
enough, theatrical etiquette is far more rigid in Soviet Russia
than in any other European country!

M. Schvezov remembers not only Danilova's Firebird, but
also her school performance of the *pas de deux* from *Sylvia*,
which he says she danced very well, her performance being
equalled only by that of her friend, Lydia Ivanova. These
two young girls, after passing out of the school, worked their
way very quickly out of the *corps de ballet* and became soloists,
by which time they were very popular with the audience,
being, in fact, one of the principal attractions of the Maryinsky
Theatre. Their very differences added to their attractions—
Lydia Ivanova, dark, short, and solidly built, had an enormous
jump and a wonderful *développé*, and was earthy, emotional,
and temperamental on the stage, giving either a very good or a
very bad performance. Alexandra Danilova, also dark, was
now tall, slim, and fragile-looking, and, as a dancer, lighter,
cooler, more refined, being very ethereal, and strictly classical
in line and technique. The contrast was extremely interesting.
What the future might have held for Ivanova we do not know,
for shortly before Dimitriev's little troupe (of which she should
have been one) left Russia, she went boating with friends on
the Neva, the boat capsized and Lydia Ivanova was drowned.

Besides her work at the Maryinsky Theatre, Danilova made
herself known by her work at concerts, mixed concerts of

D

drama, music, and dancing, and of these M. Schvezov remembers two in particular; the first, a charity performance where the dancers were Spessivtseva and Semenov, Danilova and Efimov, the two latter dancing a "*Waltz*" by Kreisler; and the second, a still more interesting occasion at the Alexandrinsky Theatre, when the State Ballet acted in a play by Ostrovsky, after which Danilova appeared all alone and danced a *variation*. She was dressed in a wine-red tunic and started her solo with eight *entrechats-six*, which produced a startling effect, and then proceeded to dance so beautifully that the house went wild with excitement and she was obliged to repeat the number before they could be quieted!

Danilova's legs were already famous, and she was well aware of the fact, since it appears that when dancing the role of the Diamond Fairy in *La Belle au Bois Dormant* she was always careful to stand in such a position as to show them to the best advantage throughout the *variations* of the other Fairies. Soon after this Danilova left her native land and it was many years before M. Schvezov was destined to see her dance again.

It was just before the end of the Maryinsky season that a retired singer, Vladimir Dimitriev, conceived the idea of taking a small troupe of singers and dancers on a foreign tour during the annual vacation, which in Russia lasted from June to September. He therefore set about collecting his artists and then applied to the Government for the necessary permits and passports. All these formalities took a very long time, including a visit to Moscow by the entire company, but at last all was in order, the visas were issued, and Dimitriev with a small company of singers and four dancers—Alexandra Danilova, Tamara Geva, Nicholas Efimov, and Georges Balanchivadze—set sail from Leningrad en route for Berlin.

Chapter V

WESTERN EUROPE

IT was early in June 1924 that the little company left Leningrad on a German boat en route for Berlin by way of Stettin. There was no send-off and no farewells on the quay-side, for at that time the regulations forbade access to the docks to any except the actual passengers, and it is certain that none of the party thought for one moment that they were leaving their native country for more than the short period of their annual vacation.

It is possible, therefore, that Alexandra Danilova thought more about what lay ahead of her than of what she left behind, and that as she sailed down the beautiful Neva and watched the golden spires and domes of the city disappear she was without regrets, little thinking that she might never in life behold them again! In any case there was excitement enough on the boat itself, for when first they entered the dining-saloon they saw, to their amazement, large baskets of bread on each table. They could hardly believe that it was all intended for one meal, for it was years since any of them had seen so much bread at one time, which must have seemed a good omen for the future!

Germany, like Russia, had recently passed through the throes of a Revolution, and Berlin as a city did not impress the Russians very much, though they were delighted with the outdoor cafés, especially in the evenings when they were lighted up, as such things were unknown in Russia, but for Danilova in particular there were other attractions. Walking down the street one day she was amazed to see a barrow-load of jumpers for sale, among which was one of shiny artificial silk in grey and orchid shades which immediately took her fancy and which she bought for the sum of three marks, after which she was inclined to think the whole city wonderful, when such clothes could be acquired at such reasonable prices![1] At this time Berlin was more or less empty owing to the summer holidays, but, nevertheless, the troupe decided to take a theatre and give a performance.

[1] Mr. Balanchine places this episode in Stettin.

That arranged for, their next requirement was a pianist who was
accustomed to play Russian music, and here they were fortunate in finding a young musician by the name of Efrem Kurtz,
the same Efrem Kurtz who is now the well-known conductor
and former musical director of the Ballet Russe de Monte
Carlo.

Their first performance being successful the troupe received
invitations to visit the principal watering-places and summer
resorts where their dancing was much appreciated, and as a
result of which they received the offer of an engagement at the
Empire Theatre in London.   This pleased them very much until
they discovered that the Empire was a music hall—whereupon
they declined the invitation, for the idea that dancers from
the Maryinsky could perform in such a place filled them with
horror.

Failing to hear of any alternative they remained in Weisbaden
for a month on holiday, revelling in being able to eat as much
as they wanted after the scarcity of food in Russia, but unfortunately for Danilova, this lazy life agreed too well with her
and she began to put on weight, which for the moment troubled
her not at all.   Finally, there came an engagement in Mannheim,
also in a music hall, but by now pride was in abeyance and
the offer was accepted.   They were just as successful there as
in a legitimate theatre, but hated working as a variety turn,
feeling that it was not suitable for the members of the Russian
State Ballet to be sandwiched in between the performing animals
and the clowns, and Danilova herself was always in trouble with
the manager for never being ready in time, horrifying the poor
man by saying that it really didn't matter if the other turns
were kept waiting.

From here they gladly accepted a renewed offer from the
Empire, and so Danilova had her first glimpse of London, which
she thought the most enormous city she had ever seen.   She was
astonished at the amount of traffic in the streets, and tried, and
failed, to count the number of cars which passed her window in
the space of one minute.   On the other hand she found the
atmosphere cold and unfriendly, and even renewed acquaintance
with the toast and marmalade of her childhood's memories failed
to make her feel at home.

In the theatre, however, she was amazed at the order which
prevailed and the speed and efficiency with which the work

ALEXANDRA DANILOVA, LONDON, 1930

ALEXANDRA DANILOVA IN "CHOREARTIUM"

was carried out, and this caused her to develop a certain sense of respect for England which was further strengthened by a visit to Hyde Park on a Saturday or Sunday afternoon. Here she heard the "soap-box" orators declaiming every sort of opinion, political and otherwise, duly protected from one another's disciples by the police, but she could not understand why a Bolshevik agitator, almost within sight of Buckingham Palace, should be allowed to implore his audience to help him to overthrow all governments. On having it explained to her that it was of no importance what anyone said so long as they did not cause a disturbance, she felt that here was liberty indeed, and her feeling towards England became distinctly warmer. She was also lost in admiration of the two-decker buses, which she still considers, the best and most comfortable of their kind in the world.

The season at the Empire was very successful for them all, but especially for her, for she charmed everyone, and was described by one very knowledgeable member of the audience as one of "the freshest and most sparkling dancers" he had seen for years.[1] The items presented which she danced were a *pas de trois*, "*Matelotte*", with Balanchivadze and Efimov, which elicited the appreciation just quoted, a "*Waltz*" of Kreisler, and an "*Oriental Dance*" from Moussorgorsky's *Khovanschina*.

It was now that she had her first Russian visitor, for one day after the performance, a lady came to her room, and after complimenting her on her dancing, introduced herself as Lydia Lopokova, and asked for news of her brother, Fedor Lopokov. Danilova was puzzled and asked her to repeat her name. She, of course, knew it was that of a dancer from the Maryinsky who had joined Diaghilev and had since danced in America and many other countries, but she could not conceive that anyone so famous and so widely-travelled could be dressed so simply. However, it was really Lydia Lopokova, and so, to atone for her disbelief, Danilova did her best to tell her visitor all that she wanted to know.

When the engagement ended, the dancers, having nothing more in prospect, were forced to think of returning home; indeed, Danilova had already received numerous telegrams from the authorities directing her to return immediately, failing which she would never be permitted to enter Russia again. However, the party were unanimous in the belief that they had not yet

[1] Mr. C. W. Beaumont.

achieved the object of their travels, which was to see the artistic work of other countries, owing to the actual holiday season in which they had to set out. They now decided that they must at any rate see Paris, and, if possible, obtain an engagement there before returning to Leningrad, as there was little hope of their being allowed abroad again. What they did not know was that Diaghilev was frantically trying to get in touch with them, but so far had just missed them everywhere. To Paris, therefore, they went, settled themselves in a modest hotel in a very unfashionable quarter, and began to look for an engagement, amusing themselves between whiles by exploring the city, which they thought beautiful, but not nearly so impressive as London.

Possible engagements did not appear plentiful, much to their distress, until one day a charming old gentleman arrived at the hotel and inquired whether they were the Russian State dancers. On being told that this was so, he proceeded to introduce himself as Pavel Georgievich Koribut Kubitovich, a cousin of Serge Diaghilev, and to inform them that his cousin would be interested to see them with a view to an engagement in his company. After some discussion they agreed to consider the suggestion, but only on condition that all were engaged together, and not only one or two of them. To this the old gentleman agreed, promising to return again to arrange an interview. This he did a few days later, inviting them to tea at the house of Mme. Sert, where they would meet his cousin and discuss their future plans. The idea of meeting the famous Diaghilev did not disturb the young dancers at all, since they knew little of his reputation or artistic achievements, owing to the difficulty with which news from the rest of Europe had penetrated into Russia after the outbreak of the Revolution, and so, this man, whose name inspired terror and respect in artistic circles throughout the world, meant less than nothing to these young post-Revolutionary dancers. To them he was merely a ballet director who might be able to give them some work.

Mme. Sert, at whose house the eventful meeting was to take place, was the wife of the painter, José Maria Sert, and renowned for her excellent taste in all matters of art. She was also one of the most noted French hostesses of the day and a great friend of Diaghilev.

When the little company of dancers arrived at the house,

which was situated in a fashionable quarter of Paris, Choura at once felt at home. Here, rather than in shabby hotels and boarding-houses, was her proper *milieu*; she recognised in the person of her hostess another member of that same world to which she herself belonged, and they made friends immediately.

Mme. Sert inquired how she liked Paris.

"Not much."

"But why not?"

"I find not very clean, and I come from clean city."

"Where are you staying?"

"Very near Les Halles (the market)."

"Well, yes, that might be rather dirty!"

And ever since, whenever they met, she would ask: "Well, Choura, do you still find Paris dirty?" To which she would answer, "Oh, no, not so very much now."

But of course the centre of interest was Diaghilev, who, with his secretary, Boris Kochno, and the cousin whom they had already met, arrived a few minutes later, and soon Danilova found herself talking with this man who was to have such an influence on her future career. He impressed her as being one of the most charming people she had ever met and very much the *"grand seigneur"*, but she was somewhat surprised at the questions which he put to her, such as what was her height and how much did she weigh, and in fact she was so annoyed that she became almost rude, saying: "Perhaps you would also like to see my teeth even though I am not a horse?"

But her tormentor only smiled and requested her to dance for him. This completed her astonishment, for in Russia the very fact of being in the Maryinsky Ballet indicated a sufficient degree of excellence to make such tests unnecessary, but she had to comply and dance, in spite of being in street clothes and shoes. She chose part of the title-role of *L'Oiseau de Feu* as she had danced it in Russia and was able to please Diaghilev very much. After the other three had passed through the same ordeal successfully they found themselves, much to their relief, engaged to join the Diaghilev company in one month's time, for the London season at the Coliseum.

There Danilova saw this famous troupe perform for the first time. Diaghilev took her with him into the auditorium to see *Le Train Bleu* with Anton Dolin in the leading role. At the close of the evening he asked for her opinion of the ballet, to which she answered: "This is not ballet as I have known it—it is just acrobatics—but the *premier danseur* is very good." Next she saw *Cimarosiana* and admired both ballet and *ballerina*. The *ballerina* was Vera Nemchinova, a dancer whose manner was cold and distant on the stage, but who could turn the most lovely slow *pirouettes* imaginable, and who was always at her best in this particular ballet (*Cimarosiana*), as also in the role of the young girl in *Les Matelots*, a part which was created for her. She was reputed to have very beautiful legs, and some busybody inquired what was Danilova's opinion about them, and she, not realising what importance would be attached to her reply, said carelessly, "Oh, they are quite pretty, but not perfection," which being repeated to their owner caused, as Danilova expresses it, "a cold wind to blow between us for some time."

The company as a whole did not appreciate the advent of the newcomers and were, in fact, even unkind to them: whether because they had newly come from the Maryinsky, or because they represented Soviet Russia, or for a combination of both reasons, it is difficult to say, but they showed their resentment very clearly, even going so far as to exclude the strangers from a Christmas party given by the company as a whole. But for this slight they were revenged a few days later when Diaghilev, in his turn, gave a party to which he invited only Danilova, Balanchivadze (or Balanchine, as he was now called), and their two companions, from all his company. But Danilova had two friends at least, Alice Nikitina, whom she had known in the Ballet School and whom she was delighted to meet again, and Felia Doubrovska, who had been in the Senior Class when she herself first entered as a pupil.

Mme. Doubrovska, who remembered Danilova as a very slim little girl, was somewhat surprised at her round full cheeks and anxiously inquired: "Have you got toothache, Choura?"

"No! What makes you think that?"

'Well, your face has got so plump," was the reply.

During this season, Danilova did not have very many roles to dance, as it was Diaghilev's custom to assimilate new dancers very slowly, so her first solo was one of the seven *variations* in *Aurora's Wedding*, and as Balanchine was free that evening she persuaded him to go into the audience, in order that he might criticise her performance. On his return he asked her: "Do you want compliments or the truth?"

"The truth, please."

"Well, you are much too fat and you danced abominably."
Danilova wept but she then and there resolved both to get thinner and to dance better, especially as Diaghilev also told her that though she was a very capable dancer she was too fat, so she proceeded to lose weight as rapidly as possible, and no one has ever been able to complain of her size since that first season.

Chapter VI

DIAGHILEV AND THE BALLET

THAT Ballet as we know it to-day would probably be non-existent but for the existence of Serge Diaghilev may seem to be an exaggerated statement; yet it is undoubtedly a true one, and to make the fact intelligible to the uninitiated it is necessary to go back several centuries in the history of ballet as a whole, and trace that of Russian Ballet from its commencement. The following synopsis is taken from *A History of Ballet in Russia* by the well-known authority, Mr. Cyril W. Beaumont.

"It is early in the 17th century, while great displays, which included ballet, were being given at the courts of the Italian states as well as before the King of France, that we first hear mention of the dance in Russia and learn that the great nobles kept troupes of female serf dancers who performed national dances before them when required. Next, a German, Heinrich Schütz, in 1673 arranged a *divertissement* before the Tsar Alexis Mikhailovich, in which a *pas de trois* and other "foreign dances" were performed, but in spite of this, it was not until 1700, after the return of the Tsar Peter the Great from his foreign tour, that dancing first became firmly established in Russia, and even then it was not "ballet dancing". Peter regarded the dance as a civilising agent, and one, moreover, which would help him in "westernising" his subjects, and to this end he gave balls at which all his guests were expected to dance, and to be dressed in the manner of Western Europe, instead of in the Russian national costumes.[1]

"The Tsar himself was a good dancer and is credited with having introduced such dances as the Menuet, Courante, and Pavane into the country. After his death in 1725, his wife, the Empress Catherine I, continued to encourage this art, which must have made rapid strides, for in 1727 the first public performances of Ballet were given in St. Petersburg. Catherine died in 1730 and was succeeded by the Empress Anna Ivanovna, and it was during her reign that a Frenchman, by name Landé,

[1] "National", but not "Peasant", for the Russian nobility had their own national costume.

founded a school where he taught girls and boys of the poorer classes to dance, and out of which he managed to produce a *corps de ballet* and some soloists. In that same year an Italian dancer, Fuzano, arrived with some of his compatriots (Julia Fuzano, Tonina Constantini, and the male dancers Tessi and Guiseppe), and proceeded to give performances using his own soloists, but Landé's *corps de ballet*, so that, almost from the first, Russian Ballet has been a fusion of the two rival schools.

"Some six years after this event, the Empress decided to build two theatres, one, the Court Theatre, for the summer months, and another for the winter, the latter being situated within the walls of the Winter Palace itself, and, as a result, Landé found himself engaged in 1738 as *maître de ballet* at the Court Theatre. By this time, Fuzano, having involved himself in some political trouble, had been forced to leave Russia, but Landé gave his ballets with a company composed entirely of Russians, with the exception of one French *danseur*, Lebrun.

"The Russian *danseuses* were Aksinia Sergeyeva, Elisaveta Zorina, and Avdotia Timofeyeva, a pupil of Julia Fuzano, and the male dancers Timoshka Bublikov, Afanasy Toporkov, and Andrey Nesterov. Landé's capacity for training dancers having been thus proved, all the financial responsibility for his school was taken over by the Government and thus formed the foundation for the Imperial Academy of Dancing, though it was not at first called by that name. This school still exists to-day as the Choreographic Technicum of Leningrad.

"The school was at first situated in two rooms at the top of the 'Winter House' where Landé himself lived, and a widow, Theodosia Kurtasova, was engaged to look after the girl pupils. The Comptroller was Captain Stepan Ramburch, who was responsible for the clothes, food, candles, fuel, and money supplied to him by the Government for the upkeep of the school and the needs of the children. In 1740 the Empress Anna died, and there was a Regency and resultant troubles, until in the next year when after a 'Palace Revolution', the younger daughter of Peter the Great ascended the throne as the Empress Elizabeth.

"Elizabeth, a very beautiful woman, liked nothing better than to dance the Russian national dances herself as well as to lead the court balls, and she gave every possible encouragement to dancers. Fuzano, who had at one time given her lessons, hurried back to Russia and obtained an appointment as second *maître de ballet*, being required to produce comic ballets while Landé remained in charge of the serious productions. Lebrun, the French dancer, was also asked to produce ballets, and these, as well as being given at the Court theatres, were shown in the public theatres without charge being made for admission.

"The two 'stars' of this period were Julia Fuzano, who enjoyed a European reputation, and the Russian, Aksinia Sergeyeva, who was extremely talented, and even in those early days each dancer had her own group of admirers, who, however, did not shout her name in the theatre, but more discreetly wore it inscribed on a small card pinned to dress or coat wherever it would be most easily visible.

"From now onwards Ballet was firmly established in Russia, and a succession of French and Italian dancers hastened thither, some to dance for a season or so, and, having taught the Russians all that they themselves knew, to return whence they came; others to remain as *maîtres de ballet* which usually meant that they became permanent residents of St. Petersburg. Among these were Locatelli, Hilferding (an Austrian whose troupe of dancers were the first to perform in Russia the *entrechat quatre* and the *pirouette*), Angiolini, Le Picq, and Canziani, who had previously been engaged to teach in the Ballet School.

"The principal *danseuses* of the period were the Russians Timofeyeva, Alexandrova, Maria Grekova, Nastasia Birilova, and O. D. Karatyghina, known as Lenushka, who was a daughter of the Comptroller of the Theatre School at that time.

"The Tsar Paul who succeeded his mother disliked male dancers and preferred their roles to be danced by women *en travestie*, and for this Birilova was by nature well suited, though she lacked sufficient strength to support her partner in an *adage*. In 1800 the first Russian *maître de ballet*, Ivan Valberg, or Liesogorov, was appointed. He produced many ballets and was joined in 1801 by the famous Frenchman, Didelot, who arrived just before the accession of the Tsar Alexander I. Didelot raised the Imperial Ballet to that degree of perfection which it has maintained ever since, and which led all the great dancers, Taglioni, Elssler, Grahn, Grisi, and Cerito to dance in St. Petersburg and in Moscow where there was also a school and a ballet company. Meanwhile the Russians observed and learnt

ALEXANDRA DANILOVA AS TITANIA IN "NOCTURNE,"
LONDON, 1933

ALEXANDRA DANILOVA IN "IGROUCHKI"

from the foreigners until two of them, Smirnova and Andrey-anova, left their country for a season and were loudly acclaimed in Paris and elsewhere, Andreyanova being compared to Taglioni in her youth.

"The last of the great foreign masters to remain in Russia was the Frenchman, Marius Petipa, who, engaged in 1847 as *premier danseur* at St. Petersburg, was in 1858 promoted to the rank of *maître de ballet*, a position which he held until his death in 1910. Many of the best-known classical ballets which we see to-day are his work, for instance, *Aurora's Wedding* (the last act of the four-act ballet *La Belle au Bois Dormant*), and *Le Lac des Cygnes* in four acts, though the scene given to-day as a one-act ballet is entirely the work of his pupil and colleague, Lev Ivanov.

"As time went on the rivalry between the French and Italian schools steadily increased, but the best exponents of each style continued to visit Russia, where the native dancers observed them carefully and added all they considered worth while to their own technique, until at the beginning of this century the Russians not only held their own, but were easily the greatest dancers in the world.

André Levinson, the critic, in his introduction to the very book[1] from which we have been quoting, makes some interesting remarks on the subject. He says "The vogue of the great Milanese *ballerine* sustained the reverberating quarrel between the two schools, the Italian, more *terre à terre*, exceeded the limits of technique in regard to *pointes* and *pirouettes*; the French strove for elegance and elevation in both the poetic and gymnastic sense of the word; and this struggle, often indecisive, between mechanism and intellect, virtuosity and feeling, aided the Russian dancers above all to realise their own value. At the beginning of the century the Russian stars ousted their Milanese rivals by combining the best of the two schools and uniting exercise to poetry and mime to pure dancing. The traditional style became regenerated, impregnated with feeling, rejuvenated by enthusiasm, exalted by reverie, without detriment to that grand air of nobility and that discreet reserve peculiar to Court Theatres."

But while the dance was thus going from strength to strength in Russia, it was declining in Western Europe. In France, at

[1] Beaumont, Cyril W., *A History of Ballet in Russia*.

the Opéra in Paris, there remained only a dead formula of the
classical tradition, while the Italians at La Scala in Milan were
more interested in the mechanics than the poetry of dancing.

In England, that country which had always so gladly welcomed the great dancers of the past, there remained only the
Danish dancer, Adeline Genée, who found herself obliged to
dance in the music halls (those being the only theatres which
continued to produce ballets as part of their programme), and
to her must be given the credit of keeping the frail dance tradition alive in this country.

It is difficult in these days of rapid communication to realise
that thirty to forty years ago it was possible for two ballet companies (in St. Petersburg and Moscow) to exist almost unknown
to the rest of the world, but it must be remembered that in those
days travelling was not so easy as it has since become, and also
that very few tourists had any desire to visit Russia, at that time
a long and dreary journey away. Those, however, whose
profession took them to either of those cities, such as diplomats
or merchants, came back much impressed with what they had
seen, but it is unlikely that those who had not seen would believe,
and it is entirely owing to the remoteness of the Northern capital
that Diaghilev, when in 1909 he brought that flame which was
Russian Ballet to Paris, was able to kindle in one night a fire
which was destined to illuminate two continents and to give
rise to many smaller fires for years to come.

Sergey Pavlovich Diaghilev[1] was born[2] on March 19th, 1872,
and passed his early years in the town of Perm. His father was an
Army officer, who was intensely interested in art in all its aspects,
and his mother was a highly-educated woman, a musician and
singer. He was educated first in Perm and then at the Mai
College in St. Petersburg, where he became associated with
Alexandre Benois, Léon Bakst, Constantine Somov, and D.
Philipov, and was introduced by the latter (who was his cousin)
to a club "The World of Art", (*Mir Iskoustva*) which he and
Somov had founded.

On leaving college, Diaghilev went to the University of
St. Petersburg, at the same time becoming a pupil at the Conservatoire. He tried his hand at musical composition and stage

---

[1] The following details are derived from Beaumont, Cyril W., *Serge
Diaghilev*, 1933.

[2] Actually in the Selistchev barracks (Province of Novgorod).

designing, but decided that he was not suited for such work, neither did he choose singing, though he had a good baritone voice, but on finishing his studies he interested himself in art as a whole. In 1897 he organised an exhibition of the works of English and German painters in St. Petersburg. This was followed the next year by a similar collection by Russian painters, and in 1899 came a grand International Exhibition of the works of the French Impressionists who had hitherto been quite unknown in Russia. The same year saw him installed as editor of the newly-produced journal of the *Mir Iskoustva* (*World of Art*) Club, which was called by the same name—*Mir Iskoustva*—and which continued to be published until 1904. The object of the publication was to popularise modern movements in art, and there were many well-known names among the contributors.

In July of this year, 1899, a new director (Prince Serge Wolkonsky) was appointed at the Imperial Theatre, and he attached Diaghilev to the directorate, at the same time appointing him editor of the *Annual of the Imperial Theatres*, whereupon Diaghilev prepared and issued a beautiful annual illustrated with portraits of actors and dancers in various roles as well as reproductions of older portraits, quite regardless of the expense involved. This was a shock to the directorate, but did not at the time lead to serious consequences, and Diaghilev gradually induced some of the young artists of the *World of Art* to take an interest in designing for the theatre. But this was followed by a serious disagreement over the production of a revival of Delibes' ballet *Sylvia*, which resulted in Diaghilev's resigning his position as editor of the *Annual* and being dismissed from the directorate, which, of course, caused the young artists also to decline to work further for the Imperial Theatres.

Diaghilev, nothing daunted, decided to prepare another exhibition, and, after travelling all over Russia, he succeeded in assembling a magnificent collection of three thousand Russian historical portraits at the Taurida Palace in 1905, as a result of which he was regarded as an authority in the artistic world and was restored to favour in Court circles.

Diaghilev now wished to make Russian art known abroad. In 1906 he produced an Exhibition of Russian Art from early ikons to works of the "World of Art" group at the Salon d'Automne in Paris, and this being successful, followed it up with a series of five concerts of Russian music at the Paris Opéra, which aroused much interest.

In 1908, under the patronage of the Grand Duke Vladimir, he produced *Boris Godounov* by Moussorgsky at the Opéra, with Chaliapin in the title-role, and Paris was enthralled; and so to the year 1909, when he brought the Russian Ballet to the Chatelet Theatre. The repertory consisted of *Le Lac des Cygnes, Le Festin* (*a divertissement*), *Le Pavillon d'Armide, Cléopâtre, Les Sylphides*, and the Polovtsian Dances from *Prince Igor*. The principal dancers were Fokine, Nijinsky, Mordkin, and Bolm, Pavlova, Karsavina, Karalli, Sophie Fedorova, and Baldina, all of whom were permitted by the directorate of the Imperial Theatres to appear under the direction of Diaghilev during the summer theatre vacation period, which in Russia lasted from the beginning of June until the end of August.

That the season was a success is an understatement for it is not difficult to imagine the effect of such vigorous male, and ethereal female dancing on audiences who were used to seeing classical *variations* performed by a girl, supported by another girl disguised as a boy. One can imagine the effect which would be caused by the wild dances from *Prince Igor*. The other Fokine ballets were also a sensation, for when *Cléopâtre* was produced, the choreography, costumes, and scenery all indicated Egypt, instead of the dancers appearing in *tutus* decorated with an Egyptian design, as had hitherto been the fashion, until Fokine had rebelled against the traditional procedure.

Paris, in fact, went wild, and from then onwards until the day of his death, Diaghilev concentrated his energies upon the production of ballet. From 1909 until 1914 he brought his company, collected from the Imperial Theatres, to London and Paris every summer, but the outbreak of war after the 1914 season made this operation difficult, if not wholly impossible, and the ensuing Revolution closed all Russian doors to him who was at once an aristocrat and an *emigré*. It was necessary, therefore, to maintain a permanent company composed of those artists who had remained with him and others whom he discovered and had trained under his auspices. Of such were Nemchinova, Idzikowsky, Woizikowsky, and the English dancers Savina and Sokolova, but later, as we have seen, he received new blood in the Russian-trained Danilova, Balanchine, and their companions, as well as, of course, some time previously,

Serge Lifar, though he was actually almost untrained when he arrived from Kiev in 1923.

Exactly how much of the success of the Diaghilev Ballet was due to Diaghilev himself is a question which will probably never be decided, though always discussed. Many books have been written on this subject, some saying that Fokine, or Benois, or some other genius was the guiding star, as against those who believe that it was the great director himself who led, while the others followed, but all are agreed that no such performances were ever seen before or since. The greatest compliment ever paid to the Ballet Russe de Monte Carlo was in Paris in 1939, when, with Massine, Danilova, Markova, Slavenska, and Youskevich, they gave a short season at the Théâtre de Chaillot and were hailed by the critics and public alike as being true successors to the Diaghilev Ballet of the first great Parisian season in 1909.

That Diaghilev himself was solely responsible for every detail of the performance being to his taste is admitted by everyone, as is also the fact of his being able to discover and develop latent talent, or, as one writer puts it, "He eminently possessed the gift of picking out talented and necessary men," and adds, "A man of great taste but unbelievably changeable, orthodox at times, and a heretic at others—at one and the same time a 'European of a cosmopolitan shade' and 'Russian, too Russian'."[1]

We know, however, that he himself personally approved or disapproved of each step of the choreography, each portion of scenery and detail of costume, and that everything which he disliked had to be changed before the ballet was performed in public, which leads one almost inevitably to the conclusion that his was definitely the guiding mind in the company. Consider also the galaxy of talent with which he surrounded himself; as choreographers, Fokine, Massine, Nijinsky, Nijinska, Balanchine, and Lifar, all, with the exception of Fokine and Nijinsky, still leading names in the world of ballet to-day; as composers, Stravinsky, Prokofiev, Poulenc, Auric, Milhaud, Dukelsky, Rieti, Berners, Sauguet, Lambert, Satie, and Fauré; while the painters who provided him with designs were Benois, Bakst, Picasso, Roerich, Derain, Matisse, Laurencin, Braque, Gris, Sert, Pruna, Utrillo, Yakovlev, Bauchant, Roualt, and Chirico.

The Diaghilev dancers were world renowned. The greatest

[1] Calvocoressi, M. D., *Music and Ballet in London and Paris.*

E

dancers of to-day are proud to have formed part of his company, while other names are merely wonderful legends to present-day audiences—Kshesinskaya, Karalli, Pavlova, Karsavina, Lopokova, Spessivtzeva, Doubrovska, Tchernicheva, Nemchinova, Danilova, Sokolova, Markova, Nijinsky, Fokine, Cecchetti, Mordkin, Bolm, Vladimirov, Vilzak, Massine, Lifar, Woizikowsky, and many others whom we see to-day. Where else could be found such a galaxy of talents?

When Alexandra Danilova first met Diaghilev she thought him a very charming man, but she knew little about his artistic attainments, for he had been too long away from his native land to have been of much importance to the authorities of the post-revolutionary Maryinsky Theatre, cut off as they were from any contact with the rest of Europe. It was, therefore, with much interest that the newcomers watched his method of managing his company, which they found in some ways different from the system to which they had been accustomed in Russia.

Diaghilev himself seldom came into contact with the individual artists, though he never missed a performance nor failed to observe the smallest detail which might please or annoy him, and upon which he would afterwards cause a remark to be made to the offender (he only praised on very rare occasions), and as a rule all his orders were transmitted to the dancers through the *régisseur*. He had also strict rules about rehearsals. Black tunics with the usual pink tights must be worn by the girls, and no unauthorised person was allowed to be present at any rehearsal, no mothers or relatives of the dancers, and when a new ballet was being arranged none of the dancers not actually engaged in it, were allowed into the rehearsal room. When each new number was ready, *pas de deux*, *solo*, or *finale*, Diaghilev would appear, watch the number, comment on it to the choreographer, approving or disapproving of certain movements, and then go away, to return some days later, when the choreography would have been changed to accord with his wishes.

Perhaps the thing which impressed Danilova most about Diaghilev after his charm, was his exquisite taste, and she will often say that it was he who was responsible for the forming of hers, for he never overlooked any detail of a dancer's toilet on the stage, coiffure, costume, tights, and even expression, and once, years later, after a performance of the ballet, *Le Lac des*

Cygnes, said to her "Your tights are too pink for the part Do try to remember that you are a swan, and not a goose with red legs !"

On another occasion during the ballet *Apollon Musagète* he requested that all tights should be dyed the same shade, and inquired why both Doubrovska and Danilova had changed theirs from rose pink to pale peach. On being told that they had found this shade gave more shadow to the legs he was pleased, but also wondered why it should have been the two dancers who possessed the best legs who had interested themselves in the matter.

It was about a year or two after she joined the company that Diaghilev began to take a liking to Danilova and to ask her occasionally to his luncheon parties, which was a great honour, as he seldom invited women. Danilova liked these invitations very much, for he was always surrounded by interesting people, and in addition, ate in such good restaurants that his parties were in every way pleasant. To this day she will say: "Let us go to such and such a restaurant. It is where Diaghilev used to take us."

Chapter VII

THE DIAGHILEV COMPANY

ALEXANDRA DANILOVA took a decisive step in joining the Diaghilev company, a step which obliged her to remain permanently in Western Europe as a Russian exile, since the period of her leave from the Soviet State Ballet having already expired, all hope of return to her native country was barred. In consequence of this she was obliged to regard the strange countries in which she found herself as her future home, and to try to adapt herself to a way of living which differed considerably from any which she had hitherto experienced. A true child of Revolution, she was at first amazed at the way in which plans were made for months, and even years ahead; seasons in London, Berlin, and Paris were booked to succeed one another in a fashion completely bewildering to the young girl, who, when asked, after the first performance in Berlin, to sign a contract to appear there again in October, replied: "How can I? I do not know where I will be then, or even if I will be alive!"

At first she was very unhappy for she found that everyone's point of view differed from her own, as was only natural, and no one knew her, or understood her well enough to be able to sympathise with her and help her, so she had to "dree her weird" alone. It was the little things which upset her most. The sight of pretty girls and women wearing lovely jewellery would induce the reflection "Oh, poor things, how proud they are of their jewels, but how very little bread they will get for it all when they are starving." On the other hand, she was amazed to find that even wealthy people with large estates were economical, taking an interest in their housekeeping and household expenses in a way that the Russians of pre-Revolutionary days had never done, for they had kept dozens of servants and left everything to them.

The Monte Carlo Casino proved another shock, for she felt, with truth, that the money lost there would feed, clothe, and house thousands. Dress did not interest her much either, as in Soviet Russia no one paid any attention to the manner in which people were clothed, owing to the difficulty of getting

ALICIA MARKOVA IN "LA CHATTE," 1927

ALEXANDRA DANILOVA AND MICHAEL PANAYEV
IN "LE LAC DES CYGNES"

any garments at all, for one would set out to buy a dresss or hat,
and return with a pair of shoes which were available that day,
while the desired objects were not. Gradually she grew to
realise that in her new life it was important to dress well but
not extravagantly, and that she need not buy six pairs of shoes
at one time for fear that there would be no more when next
she had need of them. Life, in fact, was more stable, and, as
the realisation of this grew upon her, she began to lose her fear
of the future and settle down, though it was a long time before
her taste in dress asserted itself and she could confidently decide
which fashions were just coming into vogue and which were
already on the decline.

Her first purchase had been the grey and lilac jumper bought
from a barrow in the streets of Berlin, and the pleasure she then
felt at the sheen of the hitherto unknown fabric and the soft
brightness of the colours remain even to-day in the memory
of the "best-dressed member of the Ballet Russe". Evidently
it was Diaghilev who was instrumental in developing her taste
in this direction, for before the production of each new ballet,
he would hold a "dress parade" of the costumes on the stage,
while he sat in the auditorium with his two great friends, Mlle.
Chanel and Mme. Sert, whom he always invited to assist him
on these important occasions. Mlle. Chanel is, of course, the
famous *couturière* who above all others has rescued women from
the bondage of wasp waists, high collars, corsets, and other forms
of torture by advocating the natural line of the human body and
designing dresses to that end. She it was who in *Le Train Bleu*
introduced for the first time knitted jumpers and swathed head
bands, as well as the large artificial pearl earrings now almost
universally worn. Therefore, there was no one who could
give such able assistance in the matter of costumes as she, unless
it were Mme. Sert.

Before the eyes of this triumvirate, then, the dancers would
come one by one on to the stage to hear themselves, as well as
the costumes, criticised: "So and so is too short in the leg; the
artist has designed a costume with a long waist for her; never
mind, shorten the bodice and both skirt and legs will appear
longer." In this way, Alexandra Danilova learned to recognise
every possible defect, including her own, and to learn how these
might be corrected or concealed while at the same time all the
good points were emphasised. No trouble was considered too

great to insure perfection, and the cut, throughout the design
of the costumes, was often entirely changed; this practice reached
its height before the first performance of *Apollon Musagète* for
which there were no less than four new sets of costumes.   In
addition to this, she also owes a deep debt of gratitude to Mlle.
Chanel for advice, kindly given and gratefully received; for
instance, "Never cover your forehead on the stage," or "Never
make your head look large," wise counsels which the little
Russian girl was careful to follow immediately and has observed
ever since.

Many years after the death of Diaghilev, Danilova, now no
longer a sad little stranger, was visited in her dressing-room after
a performance of Massine's *La Plage* by Mlle. Chanel, who
wished to tell her among other things that the costume she had
worn in the ballet would be improved by having a belt, and
to invite her to come the next day to her *atelier* to choose one
as a present.   After having made her choice and given grateful
thanks to the donor, Danilova heard herself called back into
another room, where to her joy she beheld Mme. Sert, armed
with an enormous pair of scissors, cutting up yards of material
and draping them on a model who stood patiently by.   All this,
however, is a far cry from those early days with the Diaghilev
company, to which we must now return.

The London season was followed by the usual return to
Monte Carlo for the Opera and the Spring season, where,
besides dancing in the operas, the company used to rehearse the
new productions for the coming year, and it was now that the
Soviet dancers became properly acquainted with the company,
and its workings, and acquired their own "roles" in its productions.   One of the soloists, Ludmilla Schollar, had just taken her
departure and her "parts" were therefore inherited by Alexandra
Danilova, but not without some small troubles.   The first role
she was given to dance was that of the Russian girl in *Contes
Russes*, which involved a *pas de deux* with Leon Woizikowsky,
who absolutely refused to partner her, saying that her name was
unknown outside Russia, and that it would lower his prestige
to appear with an unknown dancer.   Diaghilev, however, was
firm, and in the end Woizikowsky was obliged to dance, and
also to hear what Diaghilev said to Danilova after the first
performance, for he told her in front of all the other dancers
that never since the ballet had been in the repertory had he seen

the Russian dance performed as well as she had danced it that night, and in future all such Russian dances would be given to her. In addition to this, she received the role of "Estrella" in *Le Carnaval*, and the Sugar Plum Fairy's *variation* from *Casse-Noisette*, which is danced by one of the Fairies in their seven *variations* in *Aurora's Wedding*. This *variation* is now always danced by the *ballerina* who takes the part of Aurora, but, at that time, Aurora appeared solely to dance the *grand pas de deux* with the Prince. Danilova, when she later succeeded Nemchinova as *ballerina*, retained the *variation*, and so inaugurated a custom which has obtained ever since.

Bronislava Nijinska was the choreographer at this time, but she left shortly afterwards and did not return until some years later, so that Danilova's first experience of a new choreographer was delayed until after arrival in Monte Carlo. There, one day, going to rehearsal as usual, she was surprised to find in the room a strange young man in deep conversation with Diaghilev. Her curiosity aroused, she said her usual polite, "Good morning" and slipped away into a corner to inquire who the stranger might be, for she was much impressed by his enormous pathetic eyes. "Why, that is Leonide Massine," she was told. "He is from Moscow, and it is rumoured that he will do the new Dukelsky ballet for us very soon." Rumour for once proved true, and when the first rehearsal was called, all came early and were dressed as neatly as possible to impress the new choreographer. But Massine had forestalled them; he was already there, book in hand, looking just as nervous as *they* felt. He wore a strange style of Spanish trousers, which he was reputed to have adopted to hide some leg defect, and not unnaturally aroused much curiosity by so doing; though when Danilova shortly afterwards saw him dance *L'Après-Midi d'un Faune* she had a good look at his legs and was unable to find anything wrong with them, and so thought him foolish to hide them.

That morning he paid no attention to the dancers until all had arrived, but stood nervously looking at his book and making, what seemed to her, peculiar movements; then he suddenly divided them all into groups and proceeded to instruct them in the very same movements which she, for one, found very difficult to follow, particularly as at first she could not reconcile the movements with the music. After the first rehearsal she was completely exhausted, and yet had caught neither the style nor the movement. For two more rehearsals she was still "swimming in the air", then, suddenly, she began to grasp what was wanted; but, as she was always punctual, never spoke at rehearsal, and worked hard, she found that Massine seemed to regard her efforts with a favourable eye.

Danilova found him shy and very reserved, and it was years before she came to know him really well, for he seemed almost fanatical about his art, living in a world of his own into which he appeared to be afraid to admit strangers for fear that they would not understand his ideas. It was possible to disagree with him, but it was impossible not to respect his knowledge of and devotion to his art. The ballet which Massine was producing at this time was *Zephyr et Flore* to music by Dukelsky, with settings and costumes by Braque. While this was in progress, Diaghilev decided that he would like to test the possibilities of Georges Balanchine as a choreographer. To this end he requested him to arrange a Stravinsky ballet, *Le Chant du Rossignol*, for which he already had both scenery and costumes, it having been previously arranged by Massine for Karsavina, but without meeting much success.

The item which worried Balanchine in the affair was the question of the "Nightingale" itself, and it was not until he was sent by Diaghilev to the London studio of the Russian teacher, Seraphina Astafieva, that his problem was solved, for here he saw a child of fourteen whom Diaghilev had previously noted three years before, and who seemed to him to be the ideal interpreter for the role of the bird. This child, Alicia Markova, was very small, very slim, dark, and possessed of an amazingly strong technique for her years. Balanchine insisted that she should be engaged to join the company as quickly as possible, and so, in charge of a grim governess who, like the child herself, spoke no language but English, little Alicia Markova joined the Diaghilev company as its youngest member in the January of the following year. Almost the first person with whom she made friends was Danilova, who, only just grown up, was next in age to herself, and who, mindful of her own cruel reception three months earlier, went out of her way to be kind to the shy little child, though as the one spoke no English, and the other no French, conversation was a little difficult. Nevertheless, they persevered, and so was formed the basis of a friendship which has lasted until the present day, though interrupted by their separation into different companies after the death of Diaghilev.

Their description of each other in those first days is interesting.

Markova, speaking of Danilova at that time, says: "She was a very handsome girl, plump and healthy-looking, with beautiful long hair. Her expression was very serious, and her complexion wonderful, for she had a clear magnolia-tinted skin without a vestige of colour." "*Ce joli teint clair de lune,*" as another observer, the well-known dance critic, André Levinson, once described it. "Her beautiful moonlight complexion." She was always attractive to, and attracted by children, and little Alicia soon fell under her spell, or, as she now expresses it, "she was always kind and friendly, and in my childish way, even though we could not understand each other very well, I knew that I could trust her and so felt very safe with her, and when later on she taught me first the *pas de quatre* and later, the *pas de trois* from *Le Lac des Cygnes*, her word became law for me, so great was my faith in her. But it was not until after she had become a *ballerina* that I began to appreciate the full beauty of her lovely flowing movements, and to recognise the preeminently lyric quality of her dancing. Besides all this, she was kind to me in many ways; knowing that I loved chocolates and was deprived by my strict governess of those that were given me, Danilova would bring some to rehearsals in the morning, saying that she had been to a party the previous evening and had brought them back for me, sometimes adding: "But if you no dance well, I bring you no more." Whether she actually did find them on the dinner tables, or whether she bought them out of sheer kindness of heart, I never knew, but my gratitude and affection grew rapidly."

Mme. Danilova's account of Markova is equally interesting. She says: "One day at rehearsal they bring to me a little dark girl, very thin, very tiny, and I try to be kind to her, for it is not nice to be new in a company. They tell me she will be the Nightingale in the ballet and when I see her rehearse I am amaze at how she can turn *pirouettes*, and how she dance to this Stravinsky music which is very difficult—also she is the first to do *déboullés sur les pointes*, changing the *port de bras* all the time, which no one ever did before, but which now everyone copy. When she was in the *corps de ballet* she was always very exact and know just where she should be, but they could not use her there very much for she is too small. I remember also that when she have a birthday and is sixteen, Balanchine and I give her a bottle of perfume, the first perfume she ever receive, and afterwards we always give her the perfume on her birthday. Also before the birthday, Balanchine tease her and say: 'Alicia, when you are sixteen you will waltz with me,' and she get very pink and say, 'No, no, I cannot, I have already promise someone else,' and she is afraid she upset him very much."

The new version of *Le Chant du Rossignol* (*The Nightingale*) was first produced in Paris in the spring of 1926, but not without a minor crisis with little Alicia Markova. She, poor child, knowing that a nightingale is a small brown bird, had all this time been imagining herself wearing a brown gauze *tutu* and bodice of the type of the usual classical ballet costume, and so what was her horror when she found that her costume consisted of white tights, a diamond anklet, a similar bracelet, and a white cap covered with ospreys. She wept and wailed saying that she must have a little brown tutu, and neither her governess, nor Diaghilev, whom she adored, could do anything with her, and in the end it was Balanchine who solved the problem. He talked quietly with her, and explained that in China, where the ballet was supposed to take place, a nightingale and a white rose are considered synonymous, and that in this case it was the white rose aspect which had to be stressed, so that a brown costume would not be in any way suitable, and therefore, she was dressed as a rose but danced as a bird. The child allowed herself to be convinced and abandoned the struggle, but the brown *tutu* did become a reality many years later with the Markova-Dolin company, when she danced a ballet called *The Nightingale and the Rose*, where, as the scene was set in Europe, a brown bird was permissible. However, the white costume gave further trouble when the company reached London that summer, as the Lord Chamberlain did not like white tights, and so a chiffon jacket and trousers had to be added to appease him.

After the Paris season, the company visited Barcelona, next Paris again, then, after a short holiday, came rehearsals once more in Paris, preparatory to the London season at the Coliseum, after which they went to Berlin where they spent Christmas. On this tour Danilova added to her repertory the "*Blue Bird*"

variation from *Aurora's Wedding*, and joined the flock of seven
"Blue Birds[1]", all of different height and weight, who fluttered
around the head of the unfortunate Anton Dolin, the male
"Blue Bird" and reduced him to such a state of exasperation
that he shortly afterwards left the company.

Danilova, however, always declares that she was at the time
too fat for such a role, and quite sympathised with his remark
that he was a dancer and not a porter!

Spring saw them once more in Monte Carlo for the
Opera season, preceding the ballet season proper, and it now
occurred to Diaghilev to find out exactly how much Danilova
was capable of as a dancer, to which end he gave her the leading
roles in all the Opera ballets, and on a few occasions, when a
leading dancer was taken ill during the ballet season, designated
her as *remplaçant*, as a result of which he came to the conclusion
that she was a dancer who could be relied upon to give a good
performance in whatever role she undertook, and that she
possessed that most invaluable asset, a strong artistic sense.

Now came the holidays which, though pleasant, were expensive, for salaries were not high, and a holiday engagement
was always welcome. So when René Blum, director of the
Opera in Monte Carlo, offered Danilova, become Mme.
Balanchine, an engagement as *première danseuse*, and Balanchine
himself the position of *maître de ballet*, in a small company for
a season at Paris Plage, they accepted gratefully, and in this
way spent the greater part of their honeymoon, returning towards the end of the year to Monte Carlo for rehearsals, little
thinking what was to befall them and what an opportunity was
to come to Danilova.

The *ballerina* of the company at that time was Vera Nemchinova, who was just then very anxious to get leave of absence
from the Opera season in order to accept an invitation to dance
with Anton Dolin in London. After some time, and against his
better judgment, Diaghilev gave the required permission,
receiving a promise that she would return in time for the Ballet
performances. Nothing further was heard of her and suddenly
Diaghilev realised that only three days remained before a special
charity Gala at which *La Boutique Fantasque* was to be performed.
It would have been impossible for Nemchinova to arrive in
time, so the question arose of who could dance the leading role,

[1] In actual fact, the *danseuse* is not a bird, but an enchanted Princess.

that of the Doll who dances the "*Can-Can*".   Danilova was asked to try the part; she learnt it with extreme rapidity, rehearsed it very well, and gave an amazingly good performance at the Gala, much to the relief of all concerned.   While there was still no news of the missing *ballerina*, the Duke of Connaught, the brother of King Edward VII, who was wintering at Cannes, announced that he would like to see a rehearsal.   The ballet chosen was *Les Matelots*, and again Danilova was asked to learn the leading part, and again scored a success, after which came the news that Nemchinova had been engaged by Cochran to dance in a revue in London.

Diaghilev was furious, vowed that he would never take her back (which he never did), and without hesitation promoted Danilova to the vacant place, so that within three years of leaving the Maryinsky, and but five years after she had finished her training, Danilova found herself *ballerina* of the Diaghilev company.

ALEXANDRA DANILOVA IN "LE LAC DES CYGNES"

ALEXANDRA DANILOVA IN "GISELLE." ACT I

Chapter VIII

BALLERINA

WHEN Alexandra Danilova was promoted by Diaghilev to the position of *ballerina*, she was so overcome with mingled surprise and pleasure at having attained to such a high position thus early in her career, that for weeks she went about like one in a dream, and it was some time before she realised all the difficulties which lay before her.

She did, however, understand that to be given the roles was one thing, but to dance and interpret them to the satisfaction of the directorate and the public was quite another, and this brought her once more face to face with a difficulty which had beset her ever since she left Russia, and which now loomed larger than before.

At the Maryinsky Theatre both the director and the artistic director were always watching the work of the dancers, and in particular that of the younger members of the company, and the results of this supervision would be seen next day at rehearsal.

"Your *variation* was not good last night. We will rehearse it to-day and you must work more on it," the boy or girl concerned would be told, and they would be shown exactly what was wrong and how it should be corrected.

Here, in the Diaghilev company, there was not the same type of supervision, nor is there in any company to-day. Diaghilev would send word that such and such a solo or *pas de deux* had been lacking in technique or artistic expression, but it was left to the offenders to find out for themselves exactly what was wrong and to correct it unassisted. Danilova found this extremely difficult, but she applied all her intelligence, energy, and determination to the problem, and in the end was the gainer, since she acquired a great deal of artistic knowledge as well as the habit of working by herself in addition to attending the daily classes, which were obligatory for the company. She forced herself to work at those movements which did not come easily to her, and laid the foundation of a habit which continues until the present day, since no matter how long the

77

journey, or how early the company will start the next morning after a one-night stand, the slim figure of Danilova, clad in a bright-coloured tunic, may be seen any evening back stage some hours before the curtain rises, her hand on a packing-case, in lieu of the *barre*, going steadily through her daily routine of exercises.

She had very definite ideas about what constituted a *ballerina*, and certainly did not at first consider herself as being one, for she says of herself: "I just begin to be really a *ballerina* the last year with Diaghilev, and then he die and the company is finish."

The Diaghilev company at this time was, as always, a galaxy of talent of every description, and therefore the term *ballerina* in that company meant something very different from its rather loose application at the present time, when any soloist who has danced a leading role describes herself as a *ballerina* by virtue of that one role, forgetting, or perhaps not being aware, that it is not the *role* that makes the *ballerina*, but that a true *ballerina* can make any secondary part a *ballerina* role by the way in which she dances it. In America the word is used more in the Spanish sense—*bailarina*, or a female dancer, which also was the original Italian usage, since it is often used to describe a small soloist, or even a dancer in the *corps de ballet*. "So and so, a *ballerina* of such and such a company," one reads under a photograph in the paper, and later in the theatre recognises the dancer so described as one in the back row of the *corps de ballet*! To the Russians the word indicates a dancer who by her talents and hard work has risen to a position above all others after a long period of strenuous endeavour, and who, in addition, possesses that spark of genius which the others lack.

Such then was the status of Alexandra Danilova at the beginning of the year 1927 when she succeeded Nemchinova in the proud position of *ballerina*. In the company at this time as leading dancers were Felia Doubrovska and Lubov Tchernicheva. Felia Doubrovska, as we have seen, had known Danilova in the Ballet School, and had been delighted to meet her again in the Diaghilev company, and the two were destined to remain great friends from then onward. Doubrovska herself was possessed of a beautiful classical technique which she was well able to employ in a modern manner, but it was her misfortune to be rather taller than the average dancer, so that it was necessary to make special ballets for her, among which were *Pastorale* and *Le Fils Prodigue*, both with choreography by Georges Balanchine, the latter work being an enormous success both for the choreographer as well as for Lifar and Doubrovska, the two leading dancers.

Lubov Tchernicheva, on the other hand, had been in the company since its earliest days, and was a soloist at the time when Karsavina was the *ballerina*. She was considered to have the loveliest face of any of the dancers, and when in Barcelona, the impressionable Spaniards wrote articles about her beautiful eyes. She was not strictly a classical dancer, but she excelled in mime and impersonation, being at her best in such characters as the title-roles in *Schéhérazade* and *Cléopâtre*, where her beauty was shown to great advantage. She was always a noble figure on the stage, moving gracefully like some beautiful vision, and aided in all her interpretations by her most expressive hands. As the wronged young wife in *Les Femmes de Bonne Humeur* she was memorable, but she is best known to modern audiences as the heroine of the Lichine ballet, *Francesca da Rimini*.

Also in the company at this time was an English girl, Lydia Sokolova, the greatest character dancer of her day, who was frequently partnered by Léon Woizikowsky, and together or apart they created a tremendous impression. Off stage, Sokolova was a pale, insignificant-looking girl, with long fair hair, but on the stage she was transformed into something wild and elemental, as when in *Le Sacre du Printemps*, with her hair streaming behind her, she became the doomed Chosen Maiden, who danced herself to death for the well-being of her people. She was extremely musical, and to Danilova it seemed that her artistic expression found its greatest scope in conjunction with the strange rhythms of the music of Igor Stravinsky. Since she ceased to dance some years ago, no great character dancer has arisen to replace her, for unfortunately nearly all young dancers of the present time are so busy visualising themselves as classical *ballerine* that even those who have talent for character dancing deliberately neglect this opportunity of showing themselves to be greater than their fellows in this particular branch of their art.

Danilova found she had at least one old acquaintance amongst Diaghilev's special friends in the person of Alexandre Benois, whom she had known at the Maryinsky Theatre in St. Petersburg when she was still a child, and who had on one occasion kissed her on the forehead, a circumstance which she never forgot.

Now she was pleased to learn that he had great faith in her artistic sense, for on one occasion he told his son, Nicholas, in her presence, "Never worry about Danilova. She will never wear, or do, anything on the stage which is out of keeping with the role she is called upon to interpret." A great compliment coming from such a man.

The choreographers at this period were Leonide Massine and Georges Balanchine, and it was the latter who arranged the first ballet which was made entirely for Danilova, *The Triumph of Neptune*, with music by Lord Berners and costumes copied from Victorian prints of the Juvenile Drama. This ballet, first produced in London, had great success, and established Danilova firmly in her position of *ballerina*. All London flocked to her dressing-room to congratulate her, and, on one occasion, Diaghilev himself brought George Bernard Shaw, who wished to offer his congratulations in person, but Danilova was so overcome by surprise at the honour of his visit that she could hardly find words with which to thank him.

Her partner in this and many other ballets was Serge Lifar, whom she considered quite the best-looking and most charming of all the male dancers. Their introduction to each other had been propitious, for one of the first rehearsals of the Diaghilev company which Danilova ever attended, was held in a drill hall in London, which was bitterly cold, and as she sat near the radiator, trying vainly to keep warm, a young man came up to her saying: "I see you are freezing—do take my coat." Danilova, as she put it around her, cried out: "But it is a Russian coat!"

"Yes," replied Lifar, "I brought it from Russia last year. It will keep you quite warm."

Delighted to find someone who had arrived so recently from her native country, Danilova started to chat with him, and from that day they always talked together at rehearsals, and later, Lifar became her most usual partner. One day, however, during a rehearsal of *Zephyr et Flore*, she was most unfortunately the cause of an accident to his leg. She was standing in the wings, and as Lifar jumped out past her he caught one foot on her leg in passing and broke two of his tendons, with the result that the first performance had to be postponed until he recovered.

Photo : Maurice Seymour, Chicago

ALEXANDRA DANILOVA IN "GISELLE," ACT II

SERGE LIFAR IN THE "BLUEBIRD" VARIATION

On another occasion, at Covent Garden Opera House, when he was dancing the Prince to her Odette in *Le Lac des Cygnes*, he was practising back stage in the interval, and in jumping, hit his head on an iron balcony, and cut it open. He pluckily went on the stage again and got through the performance without apparent difficulty, though Danilova could see the blood soaking through his wig. His determination kept him up until the very end, when, as the curtain fell, and the Prince supposedly dies, he fell down in a dead faint and had to be carried off the stage, leaving his partner much impressed by his courage and endurance.

Lifar was always kind and helpful to his partners and very thoughtful for them, sending a bouquet to Danilova every time they danced together on the first night of a new production, a little attention which greatly pleased her. One of their performances together did, however, end in disaster, for again in *Le Lac des Cygnes*, at the moment when Odette prevents the Prince from shooting the Magician by standing *en arabesque* in front of him, her hand pressed on his shoulder, Lifar's foot slipped and he fell, so of course Danilova fell also, and Diaghilev was furious. Matters were not mended by Danilova's receiving flowers after the performance, for though both she and Lifar tried to slip away to their respective dressing-rooms unnoticed, Diaghilev determinedly waylaid them both.

"Is this what you get flowers for?" he inquired furiously. "Both of you falling about on the stage like that. What a disgraceful performance!" Yet he must have known that it was purely an accident and that no one would think of doing such a thing on purpose.

A little while after the death of Diaghilev, Balanchine was invited to produce a ballet, *Les Créatures de Prométhée*, at the Paris Opéra, but he almost immediately fell ill with pleurisy and so transmitted his views on the subject to Lifar, who arranged the ballet very successfully, and was invited to become *premier danseur* and choreographer at the Opéra, a post which he still holds, and where he has succeeded in infusing new life into the moribund classical tradition of the School of Ballet attached to Paris Opéra. He has also produced many ballets there, of which undoubtedly the most interesting is *Icare*, which has its own curious percussion accompaniment. Lifar posseses very markedly the gift of being able to convey a sense of apprehension

F

to his audience. In the second scene of *Icare* the music rolls like thunder, the stage slowly darkens, and one of Icarus's wings falls from the skies. Where and how will Icarus himself fall? The audience is tense with expectation, until he comes hurtling down a rocky slope and dies, shoulder on the ground, remaining wing and feet up, in an attitude not unlike a crashed aeroplane.

Danilova has never worked with Lifar, the choreographer, but Lifar, the dancer, was the partner of nearly all her early successes, and she regarded him as the greatest male dancer of the day. In addition, he was extremely handsome, with an unusually expressive face and body, an excellent figure, and really beautiful legs and feet. He had a wonderful way of entering into the part he was to dance, and giving it expression in the minutest detail, as for example, the role of Apollo in *Apollon Musagète*, when at his entrance it seemed that the young and beautiful Greek god had actually come upon the stage. Contrast this with the penitence of the Prodigal Son returning to his father, and the scope of Lifar's genius will be recognised. Many people in England and America have only seen him dance in *Giselle* and *Icare*, and while he makes the haunting tragedy of the second act of *Giselle* unforgettable, it is perhaps *Icare* which best gives an idea of his powers.

Unfortunately, Lifar seems recently to have acquired an exaggerated sense of his own importance as a choreographer, even to the extent of writing in one of his books that it was to him that Diaghilev looked to carry on the tradition of Russian ballet. Actually, Lifar's only attempt at choreography for the Diaghilev company was the not very successful, semi-acrobatic *Renard*, a work which could never rank with the ballets of Fokine, Massine, Balanchine, or Nijinska. It was as dancer, not as choreographer, that Lifar was pre-eminent.

Another of Danilova's partners was the English dancer, Anton Dolin, with whom she danced in *Le Bal*. He always seemed to her to be very much the young "sportsman", for which reason he never seemed able to convey emotion by his dancing. He would give a brilliant and somewhat acrobatic performance, a complete contrast to the purely classical and moving impersonations of Lifar. Conversely, in society; it was equally true that Dolin, in impeccable attire, friendly, attractive, and amusing, with his ever-ready wit, was far more of a success than the more silent Lifar. Dolin's greatest roles were in *Le Train Bleu*, and *Le Bal*, and it was in the latter ballet that Danilova on one occasion forgot her entire *variation*, and was obliged to run off the stage. Dolin tells how she started, stopped dead, stood still, and then ran off, to return only when her *pas de deux* with him started, when she whispered: "You know, I forget it all, for Woizikowsky ask me what I eat for lunch and we talk and so I forget!" As a result of that lapse she will never talk with anyone before going on the stage.

Leon Woizikowsky, the great character dancer, was another of her partners. He appeared to her to be rhythm personified, for his feet could syncopate like a virtuoso pianist's hands, and his expression lay entirely in his actual movements, so that when he stood still for a moment it was as though some of his power had momentarily disappeared. Both Massine and Balanchine as choreographers understood this very well, and Massine, in particular, kept him always in motion on the stage. In real life he was a somewhat square, vivacious little man, and Danilova liked to dance with him.

She always says, in speaking of these three, Lifar, Dolin, and Woizikowsky, that no dancer could have desired more charming partners nor more pleasant friends off stage, since all three made it their business to take as much care of their partners at the many receptions and dances to which the company was invited, as they did in the theatre.

From time to time, to Danilova's great joy, several of the Diaghilev *ballerine* of former days would return as guest artists and give two or three performances during their stay with the company. In this way, she was enabled to see some of the great stars of her childhood's days at close quarters, and also to meet them on terms of equality. The visits of Karsavina and Spessivtzeva were specially memorable to her. Tamara Karsavina, the idol of her school days, still seemed to her to be the greatest dancer of the day, as well as being one of the most charming people she had ever met. Very intelligent, with a mobile face, good figure, and perfect feet, she was as attractive off-stage as on, and was popular wherever she went, while her artistic range was wide, embracing such classical roles as Paquita (her greatest success) and Giselle, most of the Fokine ballets including the semi-oriental *Thamar*, and Massine's *demi-caractère* work, *La Boutique Fantasque*. Karsavina was the rage of Paris during the first Russian Ballet season there, and in this way she had been

one of the pioneers of Russian Art in Western Europe. Danilova was delighted to see her again and was quite overwhelmed
when she found that the great dancer was prepared to teach
her her own particular roles in *L'Oiseau de Feu* and *Petrouchka*.

On one occasion at Covent Garden, after a performance of
Petrouchka, one of Danilova's backstage visitors remarked: "I
like you in *Petrouchka* much better than so-and-so."

"Ha!" said Danilova, who does not like implied criticism
of other dancers, "and why?"

"Because you dance it as Karsavina used to do."

"Well," said the now smiling Danilova proudly, "you see,
she teach it to me!"

Another visitor was Olga Spessivtzeva, who had been in the
senior class in the Ballet School when Danilova was admitted
there. She was a classical dancer with a perfect, but cold,
technique, a lovely body, and the face of a madonna. Much
admired both in Russia and abroad, she was so fragile in health
that she seemed like an orchid in a hothouse, which one breath
of cold air would wither. In spite of her frailty, however, she
would practise so hard before a performance that by the time
she danced she had used up most of her strength, and on one
occasion carried her exercising to such lengths that she broke
her foot. Danilova believes that the performances which
Spessivtzeva gave in Russia after her return from the Diaghilev
company in 1922 were the best she ever saw, and were certainly
much better than any which she gave later in Western Europe.

During most of Danilova's *ballerina* period with Diaghilev,
the choreographers for whom she worked were Balanchine,
who was permanently with the company, and Leonide Massine,
who flashed backwards and forwards like a meteor, and she
found it interesting to work for two men whose talent took
such different forms.

Leonide Massine, whom she first met during the rehearsals
of *Zephyr et Flore*, made his next appearance to arrange a production of *Aurora's Wedding* at La Scala in Milan, and in this
gave Danilova, who was then still a soloist, a small part. Massine's next production (some time later) was *Le Pas d'Acier*, and
this was followed by *Ode*, music by Nicholas Nabokov, costumes by Pavel Tchelichev, whose first attempt at designing
for the ballet this was. It was the only ballet not actually super-
vised by Diaghilev, for he put Boris Kochno in charge and

Photo : Wm. Rader, Hollywood

ALEXANDRA DANILOVA AND IGOR YOUSKEVICH IN

"CASSE–NOISETTE"

The back cloth belongs to a different ballet

ALEXANDRA DANILOVA IN "COPPELIA"

allowed all concerned to arrange matters as they thought fit. When at last he saw the dress rehearsal he found many things he would have liked to change, but it was then too late to do so. In fact, *Ode* was a collection of experiments in lighting, cinema effects, and so forth, and while it had some really interesting moments, notably Lifar's *variation* with a rope, it was on the whole not very successful with the public, though it met with success with the critics. Danilova and Doubrovska had roles of equal importance, while Danilova's *pas de deux* with Massine was complicated by a large stick and two curtains, in and out of which she appeared and disappeared in a truly bewildering manner.

But, of all Massine's ballets, she most enjoyed *Le Pas d'Acier*, perhaps because the story was laid in Soviet Russia, where she and Massine, as two commissars, danced a *pas de deux* in the second scene. After this production, Massine again left the company, but returned once more during their next season in Italy to produce *Cimarosiana*, in which he arranged the *pas de trois* of the Greek peasants for himself, Danilova, and Lifar, and when he once again departed, his place was taken by his rival, Balanchine.

Danilova's impression at that time was that Massine, at each of his reappearances, seemed to have progressed much further along the path of choreography and to have slightly changed his style, and so she feels now that all his efforts and researches were leading him nearer and nearer towards the sensational symphonic achievements which she so much admires to-day. To the public in general, who believe that most of Danilova's great roles have been created for her by Massine, it will be somewhat of a surprise to learn that the only leading parts which he ever arranged for her were in *Ode*, *Le Pas d'Acier*, and *Cimarosiana*, all the other roles which she now dances in his ballets having been originally created for other dancers.

As a dancer Massine was occasionally somewhat absent-minded, and Danilova suffered in consequence, since, in the *pas de deux* in *L'Oiseau de Feu*, the Prince (Massine) once forgot that after two *pirouettes*, the Firebird bends backwards, and so, instead of waiting to support her, he walked to the far side of the stage in preparation for his next movement, and Danilova, bending backwards without his expected support, fell to the ground.

With the work of Georges Balanchine, the other choreographer of the Diaghilev company at that time, Danilova was,
of course, well acquainted, since she had danced in most of his
early choreographic efforts in Petrograd, so it seemed only fair
that he should be chosen to arrange the first ballet made for her
as *ballerina*, *The Triumph of Neptune*.   The name was merely a
foreshadowing of its success, for it was a triumph for Danilova,
Lifar, and Balanchine, as well as for the author and composer.   Of
course, this was not Balanchine's first ballet for the company,
since he had produced *The Nightingale* about two years previously, and in the future was to arrange a long line of
successful works to which he continues to add at the present
time.

In all his work Balanchine shows that he possesses a very
fertile choreographic imagination, which enables him to invent
many new types of movements and groupings, some of which
are very beautiful, while others are somewhat acrobatic in a
modern manner, for a desire to astonish by this modernity would
appear to be Balanchine's besetting sin at the present time, and
he seems to think that modernism in dancing is not compatible
with beauty.   This is much to be lamented, since there is a
great deal of beauty in all his ballets, and there would be more
did he not ride his muse so hardly.

"He rode a horse with wings which would have flown,
     But that his heavy rider kept him down "
writes Tennyson in one of his poems, and the phrase seems very
applicable to Balanchine in his present state of mind.

In addition to being both choreographer and dancer, Balanchine is a musician and an excellent pianist, having studied at
the Conservatoire of Petrograd after he left the Ballet School,
and dancers who have worked with him say that they can
immediately recognise that he has a true understanding of
music, and finds it easy to suit movements to the music he has
chosen.   The scope of his work is very wide, comprising as it
does such beautiful ballets as those mentioned above together
with *Le Fils Prodigue* (Lifar and Doubrovska), *Le Bal* (Dolin
and Danilova), *Les Dieux Mendiants* (Woizikowsky and
Danilova) and on to those of the present time: *Le Baiser de la
Fée*, *Serenade*, the almost syncopated *Jeu de Cartes*, the jazz of
Cabin in the Sky, and his other Broadway productions.

Anton Dolin, in discussing these ballets on a recent occasion, remarked that Danilova as a dancer was very bad for Balanchine's choreography. She was so capable that she could execute any movement required of her no matter how difficult or unusual, and he was therefore not compelled to revise his choreography and eliminate some of his more difficult movements in the way which he has had to do since, when working with less talented dancers.

A comparison between the method of work of these two choreographers is not without interest.

Massine arrives to rehearse a new ballet with the whole scheme worked out and every movement already set in his mind. This he teaches to his dancers, regardless of whether such movement suits the individual dancer or not, and he allows no deviation from his pre-conceived idea.

Balanchine, on the other hand, comes to his first rehearsal with only the most sketchy idea of the ballet already decided, and proceeds to work very rapidly with his dancers, but in collaboration, as it were, with their individual characteristics.

Massine is anxious to produce a ballet to a certain piece of music exactly as he himself has conceived it, whereas Balanchine's aim is twofold—to produce the ballet as he wishes it, but at the same time to work in such a way as to enable every dancer to appear to his or her best advantage in that same ballet. For this reason he will change a *variation* many times according to the dancer who is to take the role, and he seems able to produce many such varieties of the original dance, all in keeping with the music, without any difficulty whatever.

Again, Massine's later symphonic ballets are so complex, that many visits are needed before all the movements made by the dancers have been properly seen, while Balanchine will clear his *corps de ballet* off the stage so that attention may not be distracted from the leading dancers' *pas de deux* or *variations*, and one could go on almost indefinitely with the list of their individual characteristics, but there is not sufficient space, nor is this the place for such a discussion.

Of course, the search for the very latest thing in music, choreography, and design was always prevalent in the Diaghilev company, for Diaghilev himself had a flair, which amounted almost to genius, for picking out a budding artist, musician, or dancer, and, having once engaged them, aiding them to rise to heights which they had never before attained.

"No, this is not good," he would say. "Perhaps from anyone else it might do, but not from you. You are capable of much better things than this." The person thus addressed would retire, and in a short time produce something very much better, which would meet with the director's approval. Not only did Diaghilev thus spur them on to further effort but he would also indicate where material for their inspiration might be found, for when the company arrived in any town he would announce, "In this place, such and such a museum or gallery must not be missed," or "There is a famous statue or fountain in that park," and expected the whole company to visit the object which he had indicated. But, being human, he also knew the best restaurants everywhere, and delighted in giving luncheon parties to which it was an honour to be invited, since onlookers would remark: "Did you see so-and-so was lunching with Diaghilev? It must be true then that he has talent, or he would not be there."

Diaghilev's attitude towards his dancers was curious, for the more he admired them the more he would shout at them, find fault, and urge them to be better, while a compliment from him was so rare as to be almost non-existent. Danilova was complimented by him exactly three times during her five years in the company, which was much more often than most, but she was also cheered by hearing from her friends outside that Diaghilev was in the habit of telling people: "You know, I have a very lovely dancer, Alexandra Danilova!"

He would occasionally help her with a new role after rehearsal.

"Be more gentle just in this part, don't be too strong for this role," was his advice on one occasion; while before her first performance of *Lac des Cygnes* he inquired how she proposed to do her hair.

"Not like Spessivtzeva does hers," answered Danilova. "One must have the face of a Madonna for that." (For Spessivtzeva wore no head-dress, but parted her hair smoothly in the middle and twisted it in the nape of her neck.)

So Danilova arranged swan feathers around her head, and this fashion which she set has been copied ever since.

Diaghilev predicted great things for his young *ballerina*, and she learnt much from watching his way of directing his productions and from the hints which he gave to his dancers, for Diaghilev understood the theatre in a way which very few people have ever understood it, and he insisted that all performances should remain on a high level, never permitting concessions to the (possibly) lower level of the public taste. No member of his company would dare to turn six or eight *pirouettes* in a ballet where two only were required, since such a display, obviously intended to attract the audience, would be considered bad taste on the part of the dancer, who, perhaps unable to give sufficient depth to the interpretation of her role, sought an easier road to public appeal.

The last season of the Diaghilev company (1929) was brilliant in the extreme, including as it did the Opera Houses in Berlin and Vienna, La Scala in Milan, and lastly, the Opera in Buda-Pesth, from whence the company went on holiday, feeling very pleased with the successes which they had had and looking forward to further triumphs in the autumn. Diaghilev made a farewell speech, saying how pleased he was that they had all worked so well, wishing them a good holiday and an equally successful season next year, after which he added: "It is not possible to kiss you all, and so I will not try. But," he added, turning towards Danilova, "you, Choura, I still must kiss." He kissed her and departed. She never saw him again.

Chapter IX

INTERREGNUM

ALEXANDRA DANILOVA spent the remainder of that summer of 1929 with a friend (Agnes Peterson, the film actress) in the South of France, where she enjoyed herself very much, spending most of the day on the beach. One morning, after her usual sunbath, she returned to lunch, cheerful and happy and, taking up the newspaper, could scarcely credit what she read, for it told of the death of Diaghilev. Later, she received a telegram, informing her that Diaghilev had died in Venice. The shock was the more terrible in that she had not even known he was ill, and her first thought was to return to Paris and get into touch with other members of the company. Accordingly, she left the Riviera next day, and on the way remembered a strange prophecy which had been made to her in Paris before she left for the South.

She had given a party in her flat one evening, and a young man had offered to read hands, and to all the members of the ballet company who were present, he told the same story, namely, that there would shortly come a change in their lives, and that instead of being together, they would each have to struggle for themselves. At the time, sure of their future, and of their contracts for the coming season, they had all laughed and said, "What nonsense!" But now that the impossible had happened she looked back and marvelled at the coincidence.

When she arrived in Paris all was confusion; no one knew who was Diaghilev's heir or to whom the scenery and other things belonged, and until this was settled nothing could be done. Eventually it was discovered that the nearest relatives were in Russia, which, of course, meant that months or even years must elapse before they could be found; meanwhile, all the company realised that their happy years together had come to an end and that they must find work wherever they could.

Finally, Serge Grigoriev, the *régisseur*, remembered that the Monte Carlo Opera season would be due to start shortly. He decided to collect a small company to fulfil the contract there, and took with him Alexandra Danilova as *ballerina*.

Balanchine, Nikitina, and Lifar were engaged by Cochran to produce and dance a ballet at one of his music halls, and from London Balanchine went to Denmark, and Lifar to the Opéra in Paris.

Danilova, after the Monte Carlo season, found herself engaged by Sir Oswald Stoll to dance two ballets in his presentation of the musical play *Waltzes from Vienna*, which ran in London for a year with great success. The choreography was by Albertina Rasch and the ballets were pretty and effective. Almost immediately after she had signed the Stoll contract, Danilova received and was obliged to refuse two other offers of engagements, one from the La Scala Theatre management in Milan, which asked her to go there to dance the title-role in *L'Oiseau de Feu*, and the other from Balanchine for a musical comedy which he eventually arranged for Doubrovska and Vilzak.

At the end of the run of *Waltzes from Vienna*, Danilova, who had been parted from Balanchine some time before, took as her second husband an Italian engineer, Giuseppe Massera, who lived and worked in London, and where at that time he expected to make a permanent home. But events were taking place elsewhere which were to have a distinct influence on her future, while the death of her husband just four years later, left her once more a wanderer without any fixed abode.

During the time when Danilova was dancing in *Waltzes from Vienna*, a certain Russian exile, Colonel W. de Basil, was giving a season of Russian Opera and Ballet in London, and various other places, and finding that ballet was much more successful than opera, he decided to concentrate on collecting a sufficiently large number of dancers to permit of giving complete evenings of ballet. He therefore secured the co-operation and services of Georges Balanchine and of one or two former members of the Diaghilev company, but for the greater part of his dancers he was obliged to have recourse to the schools of the exiled Russian *ballerine* in Paris.

Thus, the majority of the dancers were very young and quite without stage experience, and even the official *ballerina*, Tamara Toumanova, was still only in her 'teens. It is not to be wondered at, therefore, that his thoughts turned towards Danilova, the young *ballerina* of Diaghilev's last seasons (reared in the strict Russian tradition of the Maryinsky), as being the one person who could help him in his present straits. To Leonide Massine, who had just joined the newly-formed company, the same idea had already presented itself, and he had written to Danilova, urging her, if it were at all possible, to join them as quickly as she could and add the weight of her knowledge and style to the training of the company.

She was hardly surprised therefore, when, shortly after receiving this appeal, she found a letter from Colonel de Basil asking for an interview at his hotel in the Aldwych. Curious and rather interested, she set off for the Waldorf Hotel and asked for the Colonel, but her surprise was great when she found herself, without explanation or apology, ushered into a bedroom where he was working with his secretary, Grigoriev, the son of Serge Grigoriev, the *régisseur* of the Diaghilev company.

The opening of the conversation also was not calculated to restore her tranquillity, for de Basil, after saying how anxious he was to have her as *ballerina* of his company, proceeded to invite her to join him as a patriotic dancer, without receiving any salary, as he was too poor to pay her. Danilova was horrified that anyone should suggest such a thing; it was altogether too much, and so she coldly informed him that she was not an amateur, that it was usual in the theatre for professional artists to be paid a salary, that she, like any other artist, needed to earn her livelihood, and therefore she could not fall in with his suggestion. De Basil then told her that he had no experienced *ballerina*, and that it was essential to the well-being of the company that he should engage one as quickly as possible, for his young dancers had no knowledge of stagecraft and lacked the style and finish of the Russian-trained dancers. Could she not in some way manage to come?

Danilova, while determined on no account to work without salary, was otherwise in sympathy with his desire to organise a ballet company to follow in the steps of Diaghilev, and quite willing to help him in the matter if she could do so, without prejudice to her own future. After some thought she suggested that he should offer her a contract for one year as *ballerina* at a nominal salary, and at the expiration of that time the question of salary could be re-opened, as by then he would have had time to make a good start. She left him to think over this suggestion and started home, having, as she says; "Many thoughts in my head".

The whole interview, from her point of view, had been

ALEXANDRA DANILOVA AND IGOR YOUSKEVICH
IN "LES DIEUX MENDIANTS"

ALEXANDRA DANILOVA AS A PAINTING BY DEGAS

rather upsetting. First, she had not liked being received in a bedroom; it was not the proper place for a would-be ballet director to conduct his business.   Second, she received the impression that Colonel de Basil was more interested in the commercial aspect of his enterprise than in the artistic side.   Lastly, his suggestion that she should dance without salary had shaken her very much.   She therefore awaited with interest the result of her proposed contract.   After a few days she was notified that her offer was accepted, and so, when all formalities had been duly completed, Alexandra Danilova set out for Monte Carlo to begin a new chapter of her career.

Breaking her journey in Paris, the idea came to her to telephone to Balanchine, who, as *maître de ballet*, could give her a little information about the company before she joined it, so she called him and informed him that she was now on her way to Monte Carlo. Balanchine's reaction was startling, he had no idea what she was talking about.   He was the *maître de ballet*; he had not invited her; and was not aware that anyone else had. In any case, no one could be asked without his knowing about it, and finally, who *had* asked her?

"First, Leonide Massine," was the answer, "and then Colonel de Basil."

"Massine!" he exclaimed.   "But I am *maître de ballet*."

"I am just beginning to wonder if you really are," said Danilova.

"Oh, perhaps I am not," answered Balanchine, and they were right, for it appeared that de Basil, displeased with Balanchine, had decided, without letting him know, to remove him from the post.   None of these episodes seemed a good augury for the future, but she was now obliged to continue her journey and hope for the best.

Monte Carlo was as lovely as ever, and the next morning saw Danilova on her way to the familiar rehearsal-room underneath the Casino where the company was rehearsing under the supervision of Grigoriev.   She passed on into the smaller room where she found Massine rehearsing *Scuola di Ballo*, with a little thin fair girl who was "hopping about like a sparrow", and who was introduced to her as Tatiana Riabouchinska, one of the three child stars of whom she had heard.

Massine seemed very pleased to see Danilova and she stayed a little while to watch what was going on before returning to the larger hall, where she sat down and took stock of her surroundings. Failing to recognise a single familiar face among the dancers, she began to study a group of women who were sitting together in one corner, talking and whispering among themselves. For some time she could not place them, for they were certainly not dancers; and it was not until she noticed that from time to time a dancer would step over and whisper to one or other of them, that she realised that they were a group of dancers' mothers.

Now the "ballet mother" so frequently written about in these days originated entirely with the de Basil company, for neither in Russia nor under Diaghilev were the dancers' mothers allowed either in the theatre or in the rehearsal-room; they were at liberty to conduct their children to the door of the rehearsal-hall or to the stage-door of the theatre and to fetch them again from the same place, and that was all. Even little Alicia Markova's mother and governess were bound by the same rule, the only exception ever made by Diaghilev being in favour of Vera Nemchinova's aunt, who was allowed to sit in her niece's dressing-room, from which she did not emerge until the performance was over!

Danilova watched the mothers for a little while and was startled to see two of them waylaying Massine on his way to the door. They seemed to be complaining about something, but Massine made his escape, saying that he would see them later.

That evening Danilova was invited to the rehearsal of a new Massine ballet, *Les Présages*, the leading roles in which were danced by Irina Baronova, Tatiana Riabouchinska, Nina Verchinina, and David Lichine. Danilova liked their work very much and thought that Lichine's face seemed vaguely familiar, which feeling was explained when he was introduced to her, for he said at once that he had met her one night when he had been an extra in the Diaghilev company and she had danced the Firebird in *L'Oiseau de Feu*, and that he was delighted she had joined the company. She also found several others of her former companions and began to feel less strange in consequence.

Chapter X

THE DE BASIL BALLET

WHEN Alexandra Danilova joined the de Basil company, she found that as *ballerina*, she would be the sole member of the company to dance the leading roles in *Le Lac des Cygnes*, *L'Oiseau de Feu*, and *Petrouchka* when they were produced, but that she had no new parts to learn at all, since the company had been rehearsing for some weeks before she was free to join them. However, it was not long before Massine suggested that she should take over the role of the Street Dancer in *Le Beau Danube*.

Many people believe that this part was created for her, but such is not the case, for the ballet was first produced in Paris in 1924 with Lydia Lopokova and Eleanora Marra, and when Massine revived and lengthened the ballet for de Basil he gave the part of the Street Dancer to Nina Tarakanova, a young girl who had been in the *corps de ballet* of the Diaghilev company during its last season, and who was now a soloist in this company. When Tarakanova started to teach her the part, Danilova did not like it. "At the end of rehearsal, I do not like it at all," she says. "I think it was little bit vulgar, and all night I lie awake thinking what can I do to make more sympathetic."

Next morning, her troubles were increased rather than alleviated by one of her old acquaintances, Evgenia Delarova, who told her that the Street Dancer's costume was horrible and advised her to ask to have it changed before her first appearance. Danilova, however, declined to do anything in the matter until she had tried it on, and, when she did so, she lifted the skirt, saw all the little frills inside, and decided to play with it on the stage. She told Delarova that she thought the dress lovely—"like foam of the sea"—only to be told that she was very foolish, as the length of the skirt was so unbecoming. "But I am not going to let it hang—I will play with it," said Danilova, but Delarova was not convinced.

"Well, we shall see," was all she said.

But before Danilova had a chance to show what she could do with the part, she became aware of something strained in the atmosphere of the theatre and rehearsal-room. She would come upon small groups of people whispering together who, when they saw her, would stop what they were saying, only to put their heads together again after she had passed, and this continued until the evening of the performance when she saw several of these little groups standing about in the wings, one of them surrounding Tarakanova, who was in tears. This was too much for Danilova, who inquired what the trouble was, only to be told it was all her fault—"You have come here to take away all our roles." To which she could only reply: "Colonel de Basil engaged me as *ballerina*. You had better ask him about it." And with that she went on to the stage for her first appearance as the Street Dancer in *Le Beau Danube*, which she danced with such skill—playing with her skirt as she had promised—that she brought down the house; and the whole company, their grievances forgotten, crowded into her dressing-room to do her honour!

But this interlude of peace did not last, and there were destined to be tears, complaints, and expostulations over every new role which she danced, for which she herself is inclined to blame the jealous and aspiring mothers rather than their dancer daughters. It seems to the looker-on rather curious that de Basil, who had been so anxious to engage her, never took the trouble to explain to the dancers at large and their mothers in particular, how essential it was for all their sakes to have one genuine *ballerina* in the company, not only to dance the great roles, but also to set a standard of excellence for the younger dancers. Be that as it may, these distressing outbursts lasted the whole duration of her stay with de Basil and were one of the causes of her eventually leaving the troupe.

The company began to rehearse *Cotillon*, and to Danilova was assigned the role of the Girl in Black, when Grigoriev one day told her that he did not know whom to give her as a partner for the *pas de deux*, and suggested that she should watch the boys at work and pick one for herself. After devoting some time to a consideration of their abilities she picked out two or three, and from these decided upon a young Dane who danced under the name of Paul Petrov, to-day regarded as one of the best partners in the world.

Massine now produced *La Plage* (*Beach*) in which Danilova danced "*La Femme Rose*," sharing it at alternate performances with Baronova, which gave rise to more floods of tears and

Photo : Lipnitzki, Paris

ALEXANDRA DANILOVA IN "LE BEAU DANUBE"

ALEXANDRA DANILOVA AND LEONIDE MASSINE
IN "BEAU DANUBE"

unpleasantness, since the mothers considered that Baronova alone should have danced it.   However, the company now put on some of the older ballets—*Le Lac des Cygnes*, *L'Oiseau de Feu*, and *Petrouchka*, and when the young dancers saw Danilova in these three great roles, they began to realise just what the word *ballerina* meant, and, as their mothers were also much impressed, there was an interval of peace.

Then followed the company's first London season, an event never to be forgotten, for the troupe opened at the Alhambra Theatre in July, 1933, for a three weeks' season, and they left in the following November, having played to full houses for exactly four months.   On the first night, at the close of the performance, Danilova stood on the stage surrounded by floral tributes, the tears rolling down her cheeks as the curtain rose again and again in response to the applause of the audience.

But if the return of Danilova to the scene of her former triumphs was one of the outstanding individual events of the season, the production of Massine's first symphonic ballet, *Les Présages*, to the music of Tchaikovsky's *Fifth Symphony*, was undoubtedly the greatest sensation, for it aroused storms of protest as well as of applause, and first made a name for the dancer Irina Baronova, who appeared in the second movement and whose best performance it then was, and, except for *Les Cent Baisers*, remains, even at the present day.   Massine followed this success shortly afterwards with *Choreartium*, arranged to Brahms's *Fourth Symphony*, certainly the most beautiful of all his symphonic ballets up to date, but this, to the opponents of the use of such music for ballet, was the last straw, and furious warfare in print began and even now continues, though perhaps Mr. Ernest Newman's articles in the *Sunday Times* did something to quell the flame of controversy.   In this connection Danilova tells an amusing story.   Seated one night at a dinner-party next to a journalist, she was amazed to hear him remark that Massine had no right to use such music for ballet—it was a horrible thing to do—so, turning to him, she inquired whether or no he had a radio, to which he replied that he had.

"Then you listen when they play symphonies?" she asked.

"Yes, of course," was the answer.

"And what do you do if they play them in the morning? You wash your face?   Perhaps you shave to them?"

"Certainly I do."

G

"Then it is you that are horrible, for Massine, he is great artist, and to all artists the music mean something—they think of love, or a beautiful country, or of happy or sad memories; but Massine, he can show what it mean to him, and that is good, but you—you shave to it. I gladly pay five shillings to see what Massine feel, but you think I pay even sixpence to see you shave? No!"

And with that she turned her back on the confused journalist and returned to conversation with her other neighbour.

"The young man he speaks no more," she added gleefully.

It was during the London season, when the different dancers went on holiday, that Danilova began to learn their roles in order to replace them, and so, she came to dance in all the new productions, and in *Les Présages* danced with André Eglevsky, it was one of his first principal roles. One of the ballets which she particularly liked was *Scuola di Ballo*, of which she always remembered the first production in Monte Carlo. The ballet is in two acts with a short interval between, but on this occasion the interval became longer and longer, so that Danilova, who had already danced in the first ballet of the evening and was taking off her make-up, could not resist going on to the stage to inquire what was causing the delay.

"The costumes are not ready," she was told.

"Not ready!" gasped Danilova, who had been brought up to Diaghilev's dress rehearsals. "Not ready! But why not?"

"Well," came the response, "Mme. Karinska is downstairs cutting out M. Massine's trousers, and she will have to stitch them before the curtain can go up."

At the conclusion of the London season, the company went on a short tour of the provinces and in Bournemouth very nearly met with grave disaster. In this theatre, the dressing-rooms are on the same level as the stage, and Lubov Rostova, one of the soloists, at a moment when she was not dancing, walked into one of the rooms to look at herself in the mirror. Behind her was a candle left burning by some careless girl who used hot black for her eyelashes, and, as Rostova turned, her dress swept into the candle flame and caught alight. Terrified, she turned to run to her husband's dressing-room on the other side of the theatre, and in her fright, without thinking of the performance, she ran across the stage, setting some of the other girls' dresses on fire as she did so. Behind her ran Grigoriev and Hoyer, both trying to catch her and extinguish the flames.   Seeing this, the musicians in the orchestra began to put down their instruments preparatory to leaving the theatre, which would, of course, have caused the audience of three thousand people to try to leave also.   The ballet was *Lac des Cygnes* and the catastrophe occurred just as the great *adage* was about to begin.

Danilova, who had seen the girl in flames run by, and who did not know how much of the theatre was burning, kept her wits about her.   Deciding in a flash that, in order to avoid a panic in the house, she must dance until the safety curtain came down, she made a sign to the conductor and continued with the performance as though nothing had happened.   In a few moments calm was restored and the flaming damsels extinguished, happily without any serious damage to themselves, but it was a most unpleasant episode, saved only from possible disaster by the bravery and presence of mind of Danilova.

Plymouth was the last stand of the tour, and from there the company prepared to take ship for their first voyage to America. They sailed on the *Lafayette*, which in their inexperience they thought a magnificent ship.   They were all very nervous since the sea seemed so vast and the ship in comparison so small, and were glad indeed when at length they arrived in sight of New York.   Perhaps none of them thought the day would come when a voyage to America would seem to be of no more importance than the journey from Monte Carlo to London.

Chapter XI

EUROPE AND AMERICA

THE de Basil Company's first view of New York was somewhat marred by the fact of their being obliged to get up
at five in the morning and put on their practice tunics in preparation for the bevy of photographers who were expected
to come aboard at quarantine. When the ship reached that
point, however, there advanced upon the dancers, well ahead
of the camera fiends, Mr. Sol. Hurok, their Russian-born
impresario, who bore bread and salt to Colonel de Basil, in a cere-
monious Russian welcome.

Mr. Hurok had for years been interested in art of all kinds,
particularly in Russian art, and was constantly engaged in
presenting to the American public the very best in music and
the most renowned musicians. He had already been the means
of introducing both Pavlova and Chaliapin to his adopted
country, and now it was he alone who had sufficient perspicacity
to realise that the time was ripe for the re-appearance in the
Western World of Russian ballet, and he determined to bring
the newly-formed company to New York in spite of the financial
risk involved, for he never counted the cost once he had made
up his mind that the risk was worth taking.

Events proved his judgment to be correct, for, since that first
year, ballet companies and ballet schools have sprung up like
mushrooms in the wake of Russian ballet, as witness to the
popularity of the classical ballet in America. But, besides
introducing the Russian dancers to New York, Mr. Hurok also
tried to make that city attractive to them, for he gave a series
of brilliant parties at which they were introduced to many of
its most distinguished residents.

It must be recorded, however, that the Russians' first impression of New York was not a favourable one. They found the
streets gloomy, dirty, and very noisy, while the hotel rooms
were dark—"like cages"—and, to their European ideas, much
over-heated. To Danilova in particular, who had never really
accustomed herself to living in a hotel, and who always regretted
the large apartment in Petrograd, it was all very uncomfortable.

S. HUROK WELCOMING COL. DE BASIL AND
LEONIDE MASSINE WITH THE TRADITIONAL
OFFERING OF BREAD AND SALT, NEW YORK,
DECEMBER, 1933

ALEXANDRA DANILOVA, NEW YORK, 1934

It will in all probability always remain a marvel to Europeans that the builders, in a country where unlimited space is available, should endeavour to cram as many tiny rooms as possible into one building, and not infrequently to design them without adequate provision either for daylight or fresh air. The theatre, when they reached it, was also small and gloomy, and having heard so much about "American comfort" they were horrified at the tiny dirty dressing-rooms assigned to them, while the theatre-manager unconsciously provided the last straw when he came in, by advising them to close the window.

"But why?" inquired Danilova.

"Someone will get in and steal your coats," he replied.

That evening, before going to bed, each dancer placed his or her shoes outside their respective doors, European fashion, to be cleaned, but next morning no shoes could be found, and Danilova, looking wildly around her "cage" could not find a bell to ring for the chambermaid! When she finally went downstairs to the office and inquired what had happened to the shoes she was told that they had all been thrown away. "And they were quite new!" she lamented. "To what kind of a country have we come?"

The first performance was undoubtedly a success, and the public was pleased and interested, even though it was obvious that the whole spectacle was new to them and that they understood very little about it. Enthusiasm grew and grew, so much so, that the company was divided into two groups, the first of which, with Danilova and Toumanova, went on tour in the neighbourhood of New York, while the second, with Baronova and Riabouchinska, remained in the city. The tour provided further instances of a different way of living, since the dancers, travelling with several suitcases as their habit was, found that in the smaller towns there were no porters to carry them, which made matters very difficult.

The most successful ballet of the season in New York had undoubtedly been *Le Beau Danube* in spite of the misadventure of its first performance. Having been warned that America had a liking for gorgeous stage costumes, Colonel de Basil decided that the colouring of *Beau Danube* would be too sombre, and so he had commissioned new dresses and ordered from Antoine's some very expensive wigs in gleaming bronze, gold, and silver, which were quite out of keeping with the style of the ballet, and so destroyed its effectiveness, added to which Danilova's wig did not fit, and fell off, whereupon, not unnaturally, she declined to wear it again.

At the next performance there was some discussion as to what should be worn, but, as Danilova puts it: "I just send them all to blazes, do my hair, and put on my old dress[1], and it is a great success!" So much of a success indeed, that the wine-coloured velvet of her dress became the season's most fashionable colour in New York.

There was a pleasant surprise in store for Danilova at one of Hurok's parties, when one night she found herself seated next to a Mr. George Somarrippa, a Russian who was now an American citizen. Being hungry, she did not at first pay much attention to him, nor observe that he was looking at her as though he could not believe his eyes, and presently, as if to make certain that he was not deceiving himself, he asked her to repeat her name as he had not caught it properly.

"Alexandra Danilova," she replied, wondering a little, but quite unprepared for his next remark.

"You know I used to pull your nose when you were about five years old," he said reminiscently.

"Well, don't do it now," exclaimed Danilova, "and please, who are you?"

"I am your cousin George," replied Mr. Somarrippa, "and I remember you when we played in the hayfields on the estate near Kiev."

Danilova found that she remembered also, and the New World began to seem less strange to her now that she found she had a relative there.

At the end of the tour Danilova, with Serge Grigoriev, Woizikowsky, Roland Guerard, and several other members of the company, about twelve in all, set sail for Monte Carlo without waiting for the end of the New York season, since they were under contract to M. Blum to appear there for a season.

The Riviera appeared to her to be more beautiful than ever, and she was genuinely glad to be back and to be able to talk to her friends there about her American experiences and most frequently about the cafeterias, which she said reminded her of nothing so much as the food distributing centres in Soviet Russia

[1] These were the original costumes, designed by the Comte de Beaumont, not the second set which he designed for Massine in 1938.

during the days of the famine! Later on she was told that they
had actually been founded on that system by someone who had
been in Russia. When the travellers arrived in Monte Carlo
they found Mme. Nijinska awaiting them with a small company
of her own, which included Boris Kniasev, who would be
premier danseur for the season, while in the *corps de ballet* was a
Jugo-Slav dancer, Mia Slavenska, whom Danilova now met
for the first time.

Bronislava Nijinska was *maître de ballet*, and Danilova was
delighted to have an opportunity of working with her once
more, for though Nijinska had been choreographer with the
Diaghilev company when Danilova first joined it, she had left
shortly afterwards and only returned some years later to arrange
the ballet *Romeo et Juliette*. In this she had arranged a *pas de
trois* for three young girls, Danilova, Doubrovska, and Tamara
Geva, but when Diaghilev saw it at rehearsal he took it out,
saying that the three danced so well that they would distract
the attention of the public from the *ballerina*! And now
Nijinska was back, and Danilova under her direction was
dancing *L'Oiseau de Feu* with Boris Kniasev, *Scuola di Ballo*
with Roland Guerard, the *Beethoven Variations*, Ravel's *Bolero*,
and Nijinska's own role of the Hostess in *Les Biches*.

Nijinska had been in two minds as to which of the roles in
this ballet to give Danilova, her own, or that of the Girl in Blue
formerly danced by Nemchinova, but she at length decided
that her own role was the more difficult of interpretation,
and so gave it to Danilova who, for her part, felt it a great honour
to become the successor to Nijinska and to Lydia Sokolova.

M. Blum, for whom the company were giving the season,
caused Danilova much amusement and not a little annoyance
by the way in which he worried and fussed over her. Since
she was the sole *ballerina*, he was desperately afraid that she might
fall ill—Monte Carlo is full of 'flu in the spring—and then
what would become of his ballet season? To this end, did
she but sneeze, he would send messengers to inquire after her
health, and as she is one of those people who can, and do, frequently sneeze ten or twelve times on end for no reason at all,
he must have lived in an unenviable state of anxiety all through
that spring.

Danilova had at that time, and still has, an enormous admiration for Mme. Nijinska, both as artist and choreographer, and

feels that she benefited a great deal from that time in Monte
Carlo. As *maître de ballet* Nijinska was very strict, disliking the
dancers to talk to each other during rehearsals and requiring them
to give all their attention to what she herself was saying. In
showing a new ballet to the company, she would explain not
only the movement which she required, but also the emotion
which she wanted it to express, and she would sometimes tell
the dancer to repeat the same movement in such a way as to
express different emotions—joy or sorrow, for instance—with
each repetition; and she would concentrate on that movement
until the boy or girl could execute it exactly as she wished it to
be performed. Though Nijinska was not in herself beautiful,
she could submerge herself so deeply in the role which she was
portraying, that she contrived to assume actual beauty while
dancing, a metamorphosis which was little short of miraculous.
Danilova always recalls with great pleasure the time when she
worked with her, and would be glad of a chance to do so again.

The season in Monte Carlo passed pleasantly and happily,
and it was almost with regret that Danilova realised that the
remainder of the de Basil company were arriving from America
for the usual rehearsals prior to the London season, and soon
that season itself was upon them.

That year, the company appeared at the Royal Opera House,
Covent Garden, where they were given an enthusiastic welcome
at the First Night Gala Performance, and the entire season was
equally successful. The new productions were Massine's
Union Pacific, which had had its first performance at Philadelphia
in the spring, and *Les Imaginaires*, a not too successful essay in
choreography by David Lichine. By the end of the summer,
the company were badly in need of a rest, and they had a holiday
in August, after which they once more set out for America,
and the New York season, which was to be followed by a tour.

It was now that Danilova received an invitation to go to
New York to resume her old role in *Waltzes from Vienna*, to
be presented there under the new title of *The Great Waltz*.
Wearied to death of life in the de Basil Company, accompanied
by the continued unpleasantness of the "mothers", she accepted
and went to New York, hoping for as pleasant a time as she had
had at the Alhambra during the year she had danced there.
Albertina Rasch, who had arranged the choreography for the
English production, was again in charge, and Danilova expected

little or no change in her former role.   But in this case she was destined to be disappointed, for Miss Rasch proceeded to change all the ballets, increasing the work of the *corps de ballet* at the expense of the soloist until there was practically nothing left for Danilova to dance.   When she expostulated, Miss Rasch replied: "You don't know Americans and I do.   What they like is *ensemble* work and not solos."   Of this Danilova was, of course, no judge, but feeling that the part was now unworthy of her, she only danced for a few days and then left the cast.

Now, on hearing that she was not working, de Basil again approached Danilova and begged her to return, for though he had done little to put a stop to the petty intrigues designed to annoy her, he was not unaware of the need to keep her in the company, and he promised her that henceforth conditions would be better.   Relying on his promise, she rejoined the company in Philadelphia on their return from Mexico City, finished the American season, and went with them to Monte Carlo.

At this point Massine tried to make life easier for everyone by allocating the roles equally, but, just as it appeared that this arrangement would bring peace to all concerned, someone raised the vexed question of first performances in each town and the trouble began all over again.

The London season was particularly brilliant that year, which marked the King's Jubilee.   Then followed the usual summer holiday before the company sailed once more for the United States, and the Metropolitan season, after which they started on a coast to coast tour, which was rendered easier for all concerned by the absence (through sickness) of Baronova, since, with one leading dancer the less, there was plenty of work for the others, and Danilova could dance all her own roles without having to fight two or more aspirants in order to keep them. Since she had not toured with the company in 1934–35, this was her first journey across the continent, and she found it most interesting, discovering several places which she liked and which she looked forward to visiting again.

First in her affections comes San Francisco, so pleasantly situated on its beautiful bay, where the charm of the Latin atmosphere of its first Spanish founders still lingers.   Danilova calls it the "Paris of the United States" and enjoys every minute of her annual stay there.   Next in her favour is the state of Florida, especially Palm Beach, which has a climate like Monte Carlo, and, finally, Arizona and New Mexico, of which she has so far had only passing glimpses during one-night stands, and which she would dearly like to explore. New Orleans, so often described as a "French City", proved to be much less French than she had imagined, though it must be admitted that the restaurants quite came up to her expectations and she enjoyed all their special dishes.

It was during the year 1936 that René Blum, following some disagreement with Colonel de Basil, withdrew himself and some of the dancers from the company, which, of course, meant that it could no longer call itself the "Ballet Russe de Monte Carlo", since that title was the property of M. Blum, who applied it to a new company which he now formed. In consequence, the company remaining under the direction of de Basil was styled the "Ballet Russe de Colonel de Basil." De Basil, of course still had the Covent Garden seasons, as well as a season at the Metropolitan, before sailing for Europe, at which two ballets were revived—*Les Noces* and *Danses Slaves et Tziganes*, both the work of Bronislava Nijinska, while the new productions in London were Massine's *Symphonie Fantastique* and Lichine's *Le Pavillon*.

It was during the winter of 1935–36 that David Lichine had asked Danilova whether she would care to work with him on an idea for a new ballet which he thought would suit her. On her agreeing to do so, they set to work, and the result of this was *Le Pavillon*, music by Borodine, arranged by Antal Dorati. Lichine always intended that Danilova should dance this ballet, so what was their amazement when, after all their hard work, Colonel de Basil insisted that the first performance should be given to Baronova.

The chief interest of the London season this year was a Gala Performance at which both Matilda Kshesinskaya and Lydia Sokolova emerged from their retirement and danced in a *divertissement* which concluded with *Danses Slaves et Tsiganes* given for the first time in London. Kshesinskaya danced a *Danse Boyar*[1], and Sokolova a Russian Peasant Dance, and then came Danilova, bewitching in a flaxen wig, her long plaits tied with blue ribbon, the leader of a string of girls—attired like

[1] National dance of the Russian nobles.

her in Russian national costumes, in soft shades of pink and blue—who wound about in a fantastic pattern, every now and then letting Danilova pass in and out under their linked arms. It was a charming little ballet, and a memorable evening.

The season that year lasted all August, the company going on holiday in September prior to an engagement in Berlin, where Danilova once again met with success, for when the season there was finished she was the only dancer from whom the stage hands requested a photograph to pin on the walls, which in theatrical circles is considered a very great compliment.

During the next New York season and the tour which followed, Danilova began to realise that many others beside herself were dissatisfied with the conditions which obtained in the company, and one day, happening to get into conversation with Massine, she told him that she was very unhappy.

"I, also, am unhappy in my present position," replied Massine.

"Why, then, we stay? With pleasure I will leave," said Danilova.

"The opportunity may come quite soon," replied Massine significantly, and Danilova felt more cheerful. By the spring of 1937, clouds had already begun to appear on the horizon, and during the following summer, these materialised in a law-suit on the part of Massine against Colonel de Basil. Danilova, expecting to be called as a witness, wrote to a friend in her very best English? "But I do not fear—I will tell the truth, the whole truth, and nothing is the truth!"

This was the year of the Coronation in London and a brilliant season for everyone, including opera, drama, and ballet, but Massine did not produce any new ballets, the only novelty being *Francesca da Rimini* by Lichine. Massine, however, revived *Cimarosiana* with Danilova in her original part, in which she looked lovelier than ever in her red, white, and green peasant dress, the whole house bursting into applause when she appeared. There was a break in August for the company to go on holiday, followed by a short autumn season in September, when Fokine produced *Le Coq d'Or*, and Lichine, a new version of *Les Dieux Mendiants*, but Massine did not return for the September season. Danilova's last performance with Massine, a week before the end of the summer season, will long remain in the memory of all who saw it.

The last ballet of the evening was *L'Oiseau de Feu*, and in the *pas de deux* of the Prince and the Firebird in the opening scene, Massine accidentally let Danilova slip and she fell on the tip of one toe and stood there in agony, utterly unable to move, for what were actually only seconds, but which to the agitated audience seemed like hours. Massine then carried her off the stage like a wounded, rather than a captured bird. There followed several minutes of Stravinsky's weird music, while the stage, always dimly-lighted in this scene of the ballet, remained empty, until, just where the music indicates that the Prince releases the Firebird, a figure in scarlet and gold flashed across the stage once more, and a sigh of relief went up when it was seen to be Danilova. How she got through the rest of the performance no one will ever know, for she herself thought that her tendons were broken. After all was over and the house had recalled her again and again in a tremendous ovation, she was found back-stage in tears, exclaiming, "Is it not terrible that now I am finish?" for she thought that she would never dance again. Subsequent investigation proved, however, that the tendon was not broken, though all the muscles were severely strained, and the ligaments torn, and it would be impossible for her to dance for six weeks.

Danilova, now that she knew she could dance again, became quite cheerful, and, with the aid of a stick, hopped about on her uninjured foot at a great rate, even going to the Opera House to see the others perform. Once or twice she managed to slip in unnoticed after the curtain had risen, but on the last night of the season, the company, waiting for the performance to begin, heard sounds of clapping and cheering in the auditorium, and concluded that Royalty must have arrived unexpectedly, but it was Danilova who was thus applauded when she entered the orchestra stalls, so much so that she was obliged to stand up and bow her thanks to the audience as though she were indeed a queen.

"I never feel so proud in my life," she said afterwards. "To think that they would do that for me."

Later, the crowd waited for her outside the stage-door and there were cries of "Oh, Madame Danilova, how is your foot?" (No foreign dancer is ever "Miss" in London, but always

ALEXANDRA DANILOVA IN "DANSES SLAVES"

ALEXANDRA DANILOVA AND BORIS KOCHNO, MONTE CARLO, 1938

Madame or Mademoiselle.) "What a pity you couldn't dance for us to-night. Get well soon, Madame, and come back."

She replied: "I am so sorry that I do not dance, but you know, I cannot help; it is not my fault! Very much I would like to dance for you."

Yet, by the beginning of September, she was back and dancing better than ever, dancing in *Les Dieux Mendiants* in such a way as to charm everyone who saw her, while on the final evening she gave a wonderful performance in *Le Lac des Cygnes*.

The company then left for the usual New York season and tour, during which Danilova found that her position in the company was getting more and more difficult. However, while she was in Chicago, she was told one day that a Mr. Serge Denham, hitherto unknown to her, wished to see her. It then transpired that Mr. Denham and some of his friends had formed themselves into a syndicate to arrange a ballet company for Massine, and that they would be glad if she would care to join it as well. To Danilova this was like a breath from the days of Diaghilev, since Mr. Denham was obviously extremely interested in all artistic matters, and it did not take her long to make up her mind to accept his offer. She promised to join the new company as soon as her present contract expired, a matter of another month or so. Her next step was to inform de Basil that she intended to leave his company. The interim was very unpleasant, since de Basil refused to believe her. He was well aware that she was entirely dependent on her earnings (since her husband had died in 1935), but he did not know that she had been asked to join the new company. He talked about giving her better roles, but although he talked in this way, in actual fact he gave her less and less to do, until, in Los Angeles, just as her contract expired, he even gave her now-famous role of the Street Dancer in *Beau Danube* to Baronova. It was the final straw—Danilova packed her trunks and left Los Angeles!

She stayed a little while in New York, meeting members of the new company which, having bought up as a nucleus the company of M. René Blum, was to be known by its name, "The Ballet Russe de Monte Carlo". The President, Mr. Julius Fleischmann, whom she met some months later, she found very pleasant and altogether charming, but it was not until the following year that she visited his farm near Cincinnati, and, finding rows of empty cowsheds, inquired why he kept no cows. He laughed and answered: "Well, you see, it had to be either my pedigree cattle or the Ballet Russe, and I prefer the Ballet Russe!"

Danilova left New York in March, 1938, and, arriving in Monte Carlo at the beginning of April, started once more on a new phase of her career.

Chapter XII

THE BALLET RUSSE DE MONTE CARLO

RUSSIAN BALLET companies (and others) have a habit of
changing their names or their "directors" half a dozen
times, and the "Ballet Russe de Monte Carlo" is no exception
to the rule.

It was originally founded by M. René Blum, artistic director
of the Casino at Monte Carlo, to fill the gap caused by the death
of Diaghilev and the disbanding of his company, and was
intended to dance solely in opera and ballet during the winter
and spring seasons in the Principality of Monaco. Then came
the decision of Colonel de Basil to abandon opera and concentrate on ballet, and so René Blum joined forces with him,
arranging that their combined companies should keep the name
"Ballet Russe de Monte Carlo", and, while still filling the
winter seasons in Monte Carlo, should tour Europe during the
summer and autumn. At first, all went well, but in 1936, as
already recorded, the Blum-de Basil partnership was disbanded,
that part which adhered to M. Blum remaining the "Ballet
Russe de Monte Carlo" while the other half was known as
"Colonel de Basil's Russian Ballet."

The de Basil organisation passed through many vicissitudes,
becoming in turn "Educational Ballets, Ltd.", "Covent Garden
Ballet Russe", and finally, that strange appellation, the "Original
Ballet Russe". René Blum's "Ballet Russe de Monte Carlo"
continued to work as before during the Monte Carlo season,
touring England, France, Scotland, and South Africa between
whiles. Among its personnel at various times were the well-
known dancers Vera Nemchinova, Marie Ruanova, Natalie
Krassovska, Nana Gollner, Nina Tarakanova, Anatole Oboukov,
Anatole Vilzak, André Eglevsky, and Michael Panayev.

Now when, in 1937, the newly-formed Universal Art, Inc.,
were seeking for a company to work under the ægis of Leonide
Massine, it was natural for them to approach M. Blum, since a
seasoned company such as his was obviously of much greater
value than any newly-formed troupe of raw dancers could have
been.

The outcome of the negotiations was that M. Blum became a "director" of Universal Art, while Massine was appointed *maître de ballet* and artistic director of the enlarged "Ballet Russe de Monte Carlo". New stars were added to the company, including Alexandra Danilova, Alicia Markova, Tamara Toumanova, Nini Theilade, Serge Lifar, Igor Youskevich, and Roland Guerard, but as Danilova's contract with de Basil had not expired at the time when the company was due to assemble in Monte Carlo, she was not able to arrive until two months later, for which reason, Massine, fearing that he would find himself short of dancers, invited the Jugo-Slav, Mia Slavenska, to dance with the company for a limited number of performances in Monte Carlo. Later she became a regular member of the company and eventually took the place of Toumanova, who left shortly after her arrival in New York to join the cast of a musical show on Broadway.

The engagement of Alicia Markova meant two things to Danilova; first, she renewed acquaintance with her friend of the Diaghilev days, and second, she was obliged to share one of her greatest roles, that of Odette, the Swan Queen in *Le Lac des Cygnes*, since, as Markova had been dancing the part both at Sadlers Wells and in the Markova-Dolin company, she not unnaturally expected to continue to do so. Another ballet in which Danilova appeared less and less frequently was *Les Sylphides*, and this was the more unfortunate in that of all those who now dance the leading role, she alone has enough elevation to give full value to the beautiful "*Mazurka*" without losing the necessary attribute of softness.

Spring rehearsals that year in Monte Carlo were hectic; new ballets had to be produced; new dancers had to learn the old repertory; and last, but not least, the new members and the original dancers had to combine and weld themselves into a really first-class company.

Massine's new productions were the Beethoven *Seventh Symphony*, *Gaîté Parisienne*, and *Nobilissima Visione* (called in America *St. Francis*), while Serge Lifar was asked to re-stage *Giselle* and to produce his own *Icare* with new costumes and scenery by Eugene Berman, which, however, were less successful than the white, scarlet and black designs used at the Opéra in Paris. The first night of *Seventh Symphony* raised very mixed feelings in the audience, but it was undoubtedly a success, and

ALEXANDRA DANILOVA IN "SERENADE"

Photo: Maurice Seymour, Chicago

ALEXANDRA DANILOVA AND ANDRÉ EGLEVSKY IN "VIENNA—1814"

it proved that the symphonic medium was the best means of presenting the talents of Alicia Markova, whose tendency hitherto towards an unemotional style of dancing was distinctly an asset in an abstract ballet. For Danilova, nothing very much was arranged, though *Gaîté Parisienne*, a not very important ballet, provided her with one of those "sparkling" roles which only she can dance to perfection, but which by no means calls for an exhibition of all her artistic gifts. Actually she did not even have the first night of this ballet either, since both Nina Tarakanova and Mia Slavenska danced it before her turn came, though when once she had danced it, it was impossible to see anyone else in the part.

The Monte Carlo season ended in May, but the company remained there, rehearsing morning and evening, and sun-bathing on the beach in the afternoons, while the management searched for a suitable theatre in London in which to give a season. They eventually leased the Theatre Royal, Drury Lane, situated on the opposite side of the road, almost a stone's throw from the Covent Garden Opera House, where the de Basil company was performing, which caused feeling among the ballet-goers to run high. The company arrived in London on Saturday, July 9th, and opened on Tuesday, July 12th, after just three days for rehearsal on the stage, which is notorious for its very steep slope. But if the dancers rehearsed all that first Sunday, the public was not a whit behind, for by Sunday after-noon, a queue had already formed, so great was London's anxiety to see the new company. Theatre queues in London are usually excellent audiences for street entertainers, and when Danilova arrived for rehearsal that Sunday, she found the crowd listening to the "*Blue Danube*" waltz played by an itinerant musician, so with a smile she picked up her skirts, neatly executed in the middle of the street a few steps of the waltz in *Beau Danube*, and then disappeared in a flash through the stage door!

On the first night, seats were unobtainable, and this rush continued all through the short three weeks' season, proving so conclusively the popularity of this company over that at the Opera House, that the manager of the latter engaged the Ballet Russe de Monte Carlo for the autumn season in September.

Only one unpleasant incident marred those few weeks, and this was at the first performance of *Giselle* with Markova and Lifar, when the curtain was twenty minutes late in rising. Now,

H

not so very long before this, there had been trouble at the Opéra
in Paris when Lifar had refused to dance at a special performance
because arrangements had been made without his being con-
sulted, and stories of this "fracas" had reached England.   The
public, therefore, decided that he was again refusing to dance,
and so "booed" him at the end of the first act.[1] Lifar, however,
took it good-humouredly, and danced the second act so well
that, at the close of the performance, cheers and boos for him were
mingled, and the auditorium was in somewhat of an uproar.
The actual cause of the delay was not Lifar at all, but the fact
that the directors wished Markova to wear the dress which they
had ordered for the production, and which she declared was not
comfortable to dance in.   For this reason, she insisted on wearing
her own dress which she had worn in the Markova-Dolin
company—hence the delay! A few days later in the London
season, Lifar appeared in *Icare*, which had a wonderful reception,
and there were no more disturbances.   In *Giselle*, too, Danilova,
as the Queen of the Wilis, excited general admiration by her
authoritative yet ethereal performance.

    After this all too brief but exciting season, the company left
for a short holiday, returning in September to the Opera House
for another two or three weeks.   During this time, there was
only one new production, a revival of *Coppélia*, which included
the rarely performed third act.   The ballet was revived especially
for Danilova, who danced the part of Swanhilda, and never was
there a more brilliant first night.   Danilova danced throughout
as though inspired, and she was given an ovation by the entire
house when the curtain fell.

    The season closed just as the shadow of the "Munich"
affair was beginning to fall over England, and the directorate,
becoming apprehensive, hustled the company on board the
s.s. *Georgic* at the London Docks, on a Thursday evening, instead
of allowing them to join her at Southampton on Saturday.
However, on the Friday morning, England awoke to learn
with deep thankfulness that there would be no war, at any rate,
not for the moment.

---

[1] This unfortunate incident had repercussions some twelve months later,
when the company appeared in Paris, for the Parisians, furious at the reception
given to Lifar in London, proceeded to "whistle" Markova when she made
her appearance in *Le Lac des Cygnes*, and a "whistle" in Paris is the equivalent
of a "boo" in London.

The *Georgic*'s voyage was one of the roughest which Danilova had ever experienced, and though she herself, being a good sailor, was undisturbed, her room-mate, Alicia Markova, suffered a great deal.   This was her first experience of an ocean crossing, and she endured ten days of horror!   However, New York was reached at last, and the first American season of the "Ballet Russe de Monte Carlo" began.   But almost as soon as land was seen on the horizon, Danilova warned Alicia Markova: "Now, remember, Alisichka, never, never put your shoes out to be clean or they will disappear!"

That first season in New York and the tour which followed were something of a puzzle to the audiences, in most cases not sufficiently well-informed on the subject of current ballet history.   Massine and Danilova, of course, were welcomed everywhere, but there were so many new names and faces to which the public had to get accustomed, even though first Toumanova and then Lifar left the company.   The tour was a triumph, however, and they had a real welcome on their return to the Metropolitan in March.

Then came a very pleasant voyage on the almost empty s.s. *Rex* of the Italian line, since Americans were at that time chary of going to Europe, so the ballet had the run of the entire boat, and very much they enjoyed it.   A seven-days' voyage brought them back to Monte Carlo, more beautiful and more dearly loved than ever, after all the strange places they had seen, and here they settled down to the thrice-weekly performances and to rehearsals of the new productions, which this year were *Rouge et Noir* by Massine, to the *First Symphony* of Shostakovich, and *Capriccio Espagnol*, with choreography by Massine and the Spanish dancer, Argentinita.   This last ballet was especially interesting, since Argentinita herself danced in it at the first three performances, and Alexandra Danilova by her own wish led the *"Jota"* in the fourth movement.   Argentinita gave her special coaching in this dance and afterwards remarked to one of Danilova's friends: *"Ah, Mme. Danilova, elle peut danser tout ce quelle veut.   Elle a les pieds très intelligents."*   (She can dance anything she wishes to dance—she has such very intelligent feet.)   That Danilova's efforts were not in vain is proved by a first-night happening.   Some Spanish friends of Mme. Argentinita were present in the audience, and afterwards went "back stage" to congratulate the choreographers.   After some conversation, one of them asked: "Who was the little Spanish girl who led the "*Jota*"?"

"She is no Spaniard," was the reply, "she is the Russian *prima ballerina*!"

"Impossible! It was a Spanish girl! No Russian could dance the '*Jota*' like that!"

But it was the Russian *prima ballerina* after all, though Mme. Argentinita had to produce her in order to prove the point.

Danilova states that after this episode, Mme. Argentinita wrote her own name on her dressing-room door as "Argentinitova" saying that when dancing with a Russian company, she must have a Russian name!

After the close of the Monte Carlo season, the company left for Florence to take part in the usual May Festival, giving performances in the huge Municipal Theatre as well as in one of the Opera houses. The outstanding event of this season was *Petrouchka*, conducted by the composer, Igor Stravinsky; and Danilova, who danced the puppet *ballerina*, came in for high praise. At the Opera House, the company performed the ballet *Cimarosiana* after the opera *L'Astuzie Femminili*, for which it was originally written, but not, alas, in the same costumes as usual. Alicia Markova and Roland Guerard, who danced the *pas de deux* most beautifully, were the only gainers, since they wore 18th century Court costumes and looked lovely, while the Greek *pas de trois* danced by Danilova and her two partners was utterly spoilt by the Italian peasant dress, which was not only too long for beauty but had a hideous "bustle" at the back, which spoilt her line completely, as well as destroying the effect of much of the choreography.

From Florence the company went direct to Paris, where they were to give five performances in the newly-built Théâtre de Chaillot, in the new Trocadero. This theatre, the largest in Paris, was completely filled every night, and both audience and critics were enthusiastic, the latter writing that the present company was worthy to be compared with the Diaghilev company at the time of its first Paris season, which was indeed a compliment.

The management was now trying to obtain a London theatre large enough for ballet performances, since this year there was a very successful play running at Drury Lane, so that it was not available. In actual fact, the company had been engaged to

ALEXANDRA DANILOVA AND MME. ARGENTINITA

After the first performance of "Capriccio Espagnole"

ALEXANDRA DANILOVA, PARIS, 1939

return to the Opera House in June, but the management passing into other hands, their successors invited the de Basil company for the summer season, but since de Basil had resigned the position of director, it was re-named "Educational Ballets, Ltd."—an unwieldy title, for, as one critic put it: "Who goes to the ballet to be educated?" Another suggestion, of course, was that if they were "educational" rather than "entertaining", they might conceivably escape the entertainment tax.

Meanwhile, the "Ballet Russe de Monte Carlo" remained in Paris rehearsing new ballets for the coming season, for the Opera management, finding that the English public were demanding to see that company again, engaged them for the September season, but only after a very amusing episode. One day in June, when the gallery public were waiting for the doors to be opened and the rest of the audience was arriving, several newsboys made their appearance, bearing copies of *Picture Post*, and calling out "Pictures of the greatest *ballerina* in the world!" —and "Danilova—the greatest *ballerina* in the world—special article!"; they quickly sold their copies to the eager members of the audience, but the management was not so pleased, since Danilova was *ballerina* of the Monte Carlo company, and not of the Educational Ballets at the Opera House! Later it came to light that *Picture Post* had, entirely of their own accord, sent its photographer and reporter to Monte Carlo in order to get pictures and material for the article, well knowing that anything concerning Danilova would immediately sell, and an American critic, hearing of this fact, remarked: "It is quite unnecessary to tell me that Danilova is popular in Europe. The mere fact that *Picture Post* thought it worth while to send members of their staff all that way just for a short article tells me that her popularity must be astonishing."

While the company thus remained in Paris, they were taking lessons from Mme. Julie Sedova, the Russian *ballerina* who had taught Danilova in the Ballet School in Petrograd, and were preparing two new ballets—*Bacchanale*, arranged by Massine to the music of Wagner, with scenery and costumes by Salvador Dali, and *Le Diable s'Amuse* (*Devil's Holiday*) by the English choreographer, Frederick Ashton. It appears that Ashton had for a long time cherished the idea of making a ballet for Danilova, and he had talked to her about this wish of his many times until now at last his chance had come. It was also his first opportunity of working with a first-class Russian company, since his previous work had been for the much smaller Sadler's Wells Company, or for the Ballet Club. *Le Diable s'Amuse* contains both mystery and gaiety, a favourite combination with Ashton, but all ends well, with a sparkling Venetian Carnival scene, and it gives both Danilova and Frederic Franklin (the hero) opportunities to show what excellent dancers they are.

The autumn season in London was announced for Monday, September 4th. Meanwhile, in Paris, the dancers were released for holidays on July 8th, with instructions to report at the rehearsal-room in the rue d'Amsterdam on August 28th. At this time there had been so many rumours of impending wars, that no one paid them very much attention, and the company was scattered far and wide, some to the Coté d'Azur, others to England or Germany, while Danilova herself went first to Central France and then to Switzerland. At the latter she had her first experience of mountain climbing, which enthralled her so much that she vowed that her first mountain would not be her last!

Chapter XIII

WAR-TIME

JUST before the news of the Russo-German Pact became
known, Danilova returned to Paris to work with Mme.
Egorova and get herself into shape for the London season, but,
after a few days, becoming afraid of what might happen, she
crossed to England, thinking it might be easier to travel there
before the holiday tourists began to return in a panic. Arrived
in London, she settled into her flat in Curzon Street and took her
dancing-lessons daily with Mme. Nicolaeva-Legat, as though
nothing were happening. Then communications between
France and England became rather difficult. No letters or
telegrams from the directorate reached Danilova, and she did
not know whether the company had reassembled in Paris on
August 28th or not. A little later, however, she heard that they
would arrive in London on September 1st; so on that day she and
Alicia Markova, whose home is in London, went down to
Victoria Station to meet the Dieppe-Newhaven train. There
they found the anxious parents of several of the *corps de ballet*,
but even though they waited to meet three continental trains,
there was no sign of the troupe. That very morning the management of the Opera House had announced regretfully that they
were obliged to cancel the season, and still more regretfully
proceeded to return the £3,000 paid in respect of advance
bookings.

On Sunday morning, September 3rd, at 11 a.m., war was
declared, and exactly thirty minutes later, there was an air raid
warning which lasted about half an hour, but Danilova, although
alone in her flat, remained quite undisturbed, for a friend, who
was lunching with her, hurried round as soon as the all-clear
signal was given, fearing that she might be nervous. All Danilova told her was "I am not alarmed. No! You see, they will
surely give the signal just for practice!" The next night,
however, when the alert was given at about 2 a.m., she did not
feel quite so brave, and putting on a fur coat over her nightdress,
she picked up her money, jewel case, and papers, went to the

"shelter" in the basement of a church opposite, and sat there for about an hour, until the "all-clear" went again. This was Tuesday, and on that morning Irina Baronova and her husband, Gerry Sevastianov, arrived in London by car from Devonshire where they were staying, hoping to collect all the stray members of the two Russian companies then in London and keep them all together until some idea could be obtained of what the directorate of each company was doing. Danilova agreed to leave London, and electrified some friends whom she met that afternoon by announcing "To-morrow I go to Turkey," and it took them some time to discover that by this she merely meant "Torquay".

Next morning, after a three-hour "alert", she departed for the West of England, where the Ballet refugees almost filled a tiny private hotel with a garden leading down to the beach. There were four dancers: Danilova, of the Ballet Russe de Monte Carlo; Baronova, Petrov, and Marina Novikova, of Educational Ballets, Ltd.; Baronova's husband, Sevastianov; the mother of Novikova; and a Russian actress married to an Englishman. Here they all remained for nearly a fortnight, receiving constant cables from America and letters from London, offers of houses for the duration of the war, and suggestions as to what they should do and where they should dance. Finally, Danilova went to London to meet Markova, and they both decided to sail for America as soon as possible, as they heard that the company would open in New York at the Metropolitan on October 26th.

After some delay, Danilova obtained a permit to leave England (which obliged her to stand in a queue at the police station—just opposite to the entrance where people had stood in rows to get into the Opera House to watch her dance!), an American visa, and a berth on the s.s. *Washington*, which finally set sail on October 1st. The voyage was long and not very comfortable, since Danilova had only an extra cot put into a three-berthed cabin, and was constantly disturbed by one of the occupants, an old lady who turned on the lights at 6 a.m. every morning, to the disgust of all her fellow travellers. The boat was delayed three or four days in Bordeaux, and it was nearly a fortnight before it arrived in New York. However, there were plenty of friends on board, for both Baronova and her husband were there, as well as Dolin, Petrov, Igor Schvezov,

and Sobinova, so they could laugh together over all their difficulties and tribulations!

When the little party of dancers eventually arrived in New
York they found the whole ballet world in a state of chaos.
The Ballet Russe de Monte Carlo was due to open at the Metropolitan Opera House about October 16th, but the date was
changed to October 26th to allow more time for the dancers to
arrive from Europe. Leonide Massine, who had escaped quite
early from France, had with him a small nucleus of dancers
from the company, and was busily engaged in collecting a new
corps de ballet with which to open the season. He was truly
thankful to behold Danilova and Markova, since *ballerine* are
not easily replaced at a moment's notice. The remainder of
the company, at that time on the high seas, actually arrived
early on the day of the opening performance, and they danced
that same night, suffering agonies throughout the performance,
since they had had neither place nor opportunity for practice
on board ship.

Henceforth matters progressed more normally. The company started on tour leaving behind most of the temporary *corps
de ballet*, but retaining the only important addition to the group
of leading dancers, in the person of André Eglevsky, who had
been living in America ever since his resignation from Colonel
de Basil's company some years previously. This year the coast to
coast tour was more successful than ever before, as was the
spring season at the Metropolitan, for which two more new
ballets were added to the repertory—*Baiser de la Fée* by Georges
Balanchine, and *Les Nuages* by Nini Theilade, the latter a charming though nebulous little work, completely spoiled by costumes
which concealed most effectively all its beautiful lines and
groupings. *Baiser*, on the other hand, was most successful,
being a triumph for the leading dancers, Alexandra Danilova,
Mia Slavenska, and André Eglevsky, as well as for all the others
who took part.

Shortly after the spring season was concluded, the company
set out for South America, landing in Rio de Janiero on May
29th, where they remained for three weeks giving performances
in the Municipal Opera House. Rio pleased the Russians,
being, as it were, a cross between the French Riviera and Spain,
while its manners and customs resembled those of Southern
Europe much more than those of North America. The theatre

itself was copied from the Paris Opéra and had one of the most enormous stages imaginable.

No Russian company had visited Brazil for ages, and the reception given to the dancers, both in and out of the theatre, was amazing. Alexandra Danilova quickly became the popular favourite, and this was demonstrated to her in a typically Brazilian manner. One evening, as she and Alicia Markova (whose popularity was second only to her own) were leaving the theatre, they found the little street leading past the stage-door crowded with people, who, as soon as they appeared, let off squibs and crackers in noisy explosions. The two dancers, somewhat alarmed, got hastily into a taxi and drove away, and it was not until the next day that they learned that to be saluted with fireworks was to receive the highest honour which it was possible for the Brazilians to pay to anyone who was the object of their admiration! Besides the fireworks, there were entertainments of all descriptions, as well as sun and sea bathing on the famous Copacabana beach, so that the company were very loth to leave Rio, and it was with no good grace that they rose early one morning and took the train for the coffee-growing town of Sao Paulo.

The journey took twelve hours and the first part was delightful, for the railway wound around the hills amid almost tropical surroundings, climbing higher and higher until it entered the valley of a swiftly flowing river. The route now lay along the river bank, and here about midday, an accident occurred, mercifully not of a serious nature. The front wheels of the engine became derailed and the train came slowly to a standstill. There is reputed to be one accident a day on the Rio-Sao Paulo line, and as this one caused no damage, it provided a welcome diversion, allowing the dancers to stretch their legs by the river's edge or along the railway embankment, where they could reach up and pick the green bananas on the trees. About an hour later, a breakdown van having arrived, the wheels were coaxed back on to the rails and the journey was resumed.

Sao Paulo proved to be a commercial city of distinctly German tendencies, in strong contrast to Rio where the atmosphere is very French, and it also possessed a really magnificent theatre with the most wonderful dressing-rooms for the dancers— parquet floors and white paint! Here Danilova met again Mme. Gulzgova, who, as Vera Timé, had been her fellow pupil

in the Ballet School, and who was now married and living in
Sao Paulo.   The world-famous Snake Farm and Museum were
of course visited, and, as a result, the dancers suffered from acute
nightmare for some time afterwards.   Nerve-racking, too, was
the journey to Santos, which involved a funicular-like descent
from the top of the mountains to the marshy plain, almost level
with the sea, which surrounded the town.   The ascent and
descent had to be made twice, once in order to give a performance
in Santos and the second time to go on board the boat for Buenos
Aires.   Santos itself, backed by deep blue mountains, suggests
a Japanese print.   Town, river, and fields are a quiet, greenish-
grey; there is none of the vividly arresting beauty of Rio, but it
is charming none the less.

Both Montevideo and Buenos Aires seemed colourless in
comparison with Brazil, but on further acquaintance proved
delightful, while the food in the Argentine will long remain
in the memory of the Ballet Russe.

"Do you remember the 'Chateaubriand' in Buenos Aires?"
you will hear them ask.   "So thick, so juicy, and all for twenty
cents!"

It was on the voyage from New York and afterwards in
Rio de Janeiro that Alexandra Danilova first started to give
regular dancing-lessons to the company, and proved herself to be
such an excellent teacher that even the laziest dancers bestirred
themselves in the early morning so as to be in time for her
classes.   Rehearsals, too, were going on apace for the new autumn
season productions, and so urgent did this matter become that
no holidays were considered possible for the company, with the
exception of what rest they could obtain during the seventeen-
day voyage back to New York.

When at length the Ballet season opened, it was not at the
Metropolitan, which was being renovated, but at the much
smaller 51st Street Theatre, where New York audiences got their
first chance of seeing ballet at close quarters.   The new ballets
were *Vienna*—1814, and *The New Yorker*, both by Leonide
Massine, a revival of *Casse-Noisette* by Alexandra Fedorova,
Jeu de Cartes (*Poker Game*), and *Serenade*, both by Georges
Balanchine.

Danilova danced the leading role, or rather, two roles, in
Vienna, since she appears first as one of the *Débutantes*, and
secondly, as the Spirit of France, complete with *bonnet rouge*

and diamond tiara. The costume is most becoming and her dancing is excellent.

"I remember chiefly Danilova's twinkling silken legs," wrote one of the critics, and indeed they are well worth remembering.

In *Poker Game*, both Markova and Danilova, as the Queens of Hearts and Spades respectively, found themselves dancing jazz *sur les pointes* with much success and to their own great amusement. *Serenade*, a particularly lovely ballet, was not shown to its best advantage in New York, since it was danced by the American, Marie Jeanne, as guest artist, and it was an unfortunate idea for an American dancer to appear with a Russian company in the most Russian ballet by a Russian choreographer to the music of Tchaikovsky! The full beauty of *Serenade* was only revealed during the tour, when Danilova and Krassovska danced the leading parts alternately.

Following this New York season came the usual coast to coast tour. To the dancers it was monotonous since, owing to the popularity of three of the ballets, the programme frequently consisted of *Serenade*, *Casse-Noisette*, and *Capriccio Espagnol*, which combination soon became disrespectfully known as "Ham and Eggs".

During this time Danilova found herself dancing in fewer and fewer of the classical ballets, these roles being divided between Markova and Slavenska, until the Christmas season in Chicago, when the public demand for Danilova's appearance in *Le Lac des Cygnes* grew too insistent to be disregarded. The resultant performance was so exquisite and so much acclaimed by critics and public alike, that the "powers that be" were some-what forcibly obliged to recall to mind the fact that Danilova is, before everything else, a classical dancer.

But Danilova provided another surprise for the company and public alike, when, during a performance at Claremont, California, early in February, she announced that she and Casimir Kokich (one of the soloists) had that morning applied for a marriage licence and that the ceremony itself would take place on St. Valentine's Day in Los Angeles.

The wedding was a quiet one, only six people besides the bride and bridegroom being present. Danilova looked very pretty in green and beige and carried a bouquet of gardenias and white gladiolas. After the ceremony, Mr. Denham, Vice-President of Universal Art, Inc., gave a luncheon-party for the

IRINA BARONOVA, ALEXANDRA DANILOVA, G. SEVASTIANOV, AND PAUL PETROV, TORQUAY, 1939

ALEXANDRA DANILOVA AND ALICIA MARKOVA, PARIS, 1939

Markova   Danilova

newly-married pair, for which he himself cooked the appropriate Russian dishes.

That evening Danilova danced the role of the Bride in *Baiser de la Fée* and the audience went wild with excitement. She was recalled again and again to a stage covered from end to end with flowers; in fact, there were so many bouquets that some of the cards attached fell off and were never found, so that the donors could not be thanked for their charming offerings. Danilova's wedding was the fourth which had occurred in the company within eight months, the first being that of Nini Theilade to Mr. Peter de Loopuyt, whom she met in Rio de Janeiro and married in Montevideo, he having in the interval followed the company to Buenos Aires.

Once back in New York an important change took place in the composition of the company, for Alicia Markova, whose contract had now terminated, announced her intention of rejoining Anton Dolin, her former partner, who was working with the "Ballet Theatre", a recently-formed American company. Everyone regretted her departure and did their best to persuade her to change her mind, but without avail. Her place was taken by Tamara Toumanova.

Toumanova, beautiful as ever and much thinner, had recently been with the de Basil ballet, and was the brightest star of their Australian and American seasons. She took over all Markova's roles to which she added one of Nini Theilade's, the slow movement of the Beethoven *Seventh Symphony*, which she danced to perfection.

Another short tour in the southern states followed immediately, after which the company were set free for some six or eight weeks' holiday, their first for almost two years. Early June saw them back in New York, combating a heat-wave and preparing for a series of performances at the Lewisohn Stadium. For the first group of evenings, the weather was propitious, and the attendance enormous, but during the second week, the heat-wave broke in a torrential downpour during the first interval and the audience was forced to seek shelter wherever it could be found.

Danilova, already dressed for her role in *Petrouchka* which was second on the programme, opened the door of the little wooden shed which was her dressing-room and discovered two small children crouching beside it in the vain hope of being protected from the rain. She quickly clapped them both inside, removed their wet coats, shoes and stockings, and started to massage their cold feet with eau-de-Cologne. The two little girls thought it great fun and, when fitted out with Danilova's practice socks, were overjoyed, since they would be obliged to come backstage another night in order to return them to their proper owner.

The next engagement was for another series of open-air performances, this time in the Hollywood Bowl. On the way the company stopped for two nights in San Antonio, Texas, to dance in the Sunken Garden Theatre in Breckenridge Park, just outside the town.

Of all open air theatres this must surely be one of the loveliest, possessing as it does a natural background of rocky hill embellished with trees and shrubs, a winding pathway, and a little tinkling waterfall. Here *Les Sylphides* and *Le Lac des Cygnes* took on a dreamlike quality (if one excepts the huge flying crickets which were far too real for the dancers' comfort), but the best of all was *Le Beau Danube*. By some curious trick of lighting all the trees took on autumn tints, thus harmonising perfectly with Danilova's chestnut-brown velvet dress, and producing a perfect picture.

Jean Yasvinsky, the *régisseur*, was enthralled by it, and, meeting the writer, inquired:

"You see this from front? No? Then you come now with me, for never will you see again this ballet so beautiful!" It must be admitted that the effect was really lovely.

After all this beauty, the enormous empty metal shell of the Hollywood Bowl seemed singularly uninspired, while the absence of proper "wings" spoilt the effect of many of the ballets, since the characters were obliged to make their entrance or exit either at the centre back or else through a small door at the edge of the stage on either side.

The auditorium was enormous, holding 21,000 people, and it was completely filled for the ballet, thus winning a silver cup for Mr. Hurok, since it was his entertainment which had made the record for the season.

A week's engagement at the San Francisco Opera House followed and then another performance in the Bowl, before a new venture was embarked on.

This was the filming of two ballets, *Gaîté Parisienne* and

Capriccio Espagnol at Warner Brothers Studio, and was something in the nature of an experiment. The first tests were announced as being for *Capriccio Espagnol* and the dancers summoned were Alexandra Danilova, Tamara Toumanova, Natalie Krassovska, and a Czech-American soloist, Mlada Mladova.

The test having been completed, the film director who had previously met all the company in San Francisco, turned to Danilova and asked if she could get ready for *Gaîté Parisienne*. Danilova answered that she had been told only that morning to prepare for the Spanish ballet, and therefore she had neither tights, ballet shoes, nor the necessary items for the very elaborate coiffure required.

"It doesn't matter," was the answer, "we will see if your costume is here." It was there, and so Danilova was dressed, and her hair, instead of being becomingly arranged in soft curls, was pulled up on the top of her head in a fashion which would have been trying to Venus herself. In this guise she was obliged to undergo an almost static test for her famous role of the Glove-Seller, since, having no ballet-shoes, she could not dance it properly. In the meantime, Mladova was being dressed in the most becoming costume available (in *Gaîté* she normally danced in the *corps de ballet*) and her head wreathed with flowers. She also was tested.

Later on, Danilova inquired about the results and was told, "the cast for *Gaîté* is not yet decided, as we must change the ballet before it is filmed. The Glove-Seller must be young and innocent, and have a very pretty face." Danilova replied to the effect that Frenchwomen are usually chic, witty, and charming rather than pretty, and that, in any case, the Glove-Seller was definitely sophisticated, and had been long enough in the café for her fame to have reached the Baron in Vienna.

"We are going to change all that," she was told; "the film public must have pretty and innocent heroines." Later came the news that Mladova was to have the part, since she was very pretty and apparently photogenic.

Feeling in the company ran very high and resentment was not mitigated when it transpired that Danilova had been asked to teach her role to Mladova. Danilova herself said very little. She took great pains to teach the part and awaited the result with interest.

The film was a bitter disappointment to all who were

familiar with the ballet as given on the stage. The pretty little Glove-Seller smiled very sweetly but her performance had little of the sparkle of Danilova's interpretation, and so the famous waltz which brings the house down had to be reduced to a few shots reflected in miniature in a mirror, and to the final pose as the music ends.

The film director had not realised that no soloist, however good she may be in her own degree, is able to dance a role created for a *ballerina*. A good film director may be able to make an actress out of a pretty newcomer but to make a *ballerina* out of a soloist in six weeks is an impossibility.

That his choice fell upon Mlada Mladova was unfair to her also, since even had she possessed the technique, and experience required, she was quite unsuited to that type of part. Mladova is at her best in rather melancholy and moonlight roles. Her *"Prélude"* in *Les Sylphides* is charming, and so is her rendering of the Girl in Blue in the *adage* of Balanchine's ballet, *Serenade*. Her movements are slow and graceful and her personality is appealing rather than compelling. She is the very reverse of the heartless charmer of *Gaîté Parisienne* or the *Gay Parisian* as the film is called.

That Danilova is not only photogenic, but can give a good account of herself in the movies, is proved by her excellent performance in *Spanish Fiesta* (*Capriccio Espagnol*) where, with the exception of the substitution of Toumanova for Krassovska, and the interpolation of a new role for the latter, as well as one for Franklin, the stage and screen castes are the same.

Leaving Hollywood, the company set out for Canada, stopping *en route* for a performance in Denver, where Danilova made her first appearance in *Schéhérazade*, and so stimulated the company that Massine afterwards remarked that it was the "gayest *Schéhérazade* he had ever witnessed."

The next week in Toronto saw her first performance of *Casse-Noisette*, for a description of which we cannot do better than quote Yasvinsky's remarks on his return to New York:

"What for you no go to Canada? You miss something—Choura in *Casse Noisette*. She was"—here words failed him and he blew a kiss towards the roof—"but wonderful, wonderful. The real Russian *ballerina*. You must be sorry, very sorry that you do not see."

Other members of the company confirmed his statement,

EN ROUTE TO RIO DE JANEIRO

J. Yasvinsky, Mrs. S. Hurok, Mia Slavenska, Alexandra Danilova, S. Hurok, Alicia Markova

ALEXANDRA DANILOVA, RIO DE JANEIRO, JUNE, 1940

Photo: Jorge de Castro

saying that they themselves had stood in the wings applauding as the curtain fell.

The subsequent New York season was a nightmare by reason of the rehearsals required for the three new productions, Massine's *Labyrinth*, and *Saratoga*, and Alexandra Fedorova's reconstruction of Petipa's ballroom scene in *Le Lac des Cygnes*, under the title of *The Magic Swan*. Rehearsals continued after the performances, sometimes until 3 a.m.; and by the time the tour started, the company were already completely exhausted.

The tour was longer and more successful than ever before, and it was a major triumph for Danilova, and for her usual partner, Igor Youskevich, who bore the brunt of all the classical work, as Eglevsky had met with an injury to his knee. Danilova found herself hailed everywhere as the greatest classical dancer of the present day, this being the first time that American audiences had been given an opportunity of seeing her in purely classical roles. That year her repertory included two acts of *Le Lac des Cygnes* (*Swan Lake* and *The Magic Swan*), *Casse-Noisette*, *Coppélia*, and two modern classical ballets, Massine's *Vienna*—1814 and Balanchine's *Serenade*.

Danilova deserves all the success she has achieved—she has struggled through difficulties and disasters against the jealousy of some of her fellow artistes without becoming either jealous or embittered herself, for she firmly believes in the Russian saying:

"Do not go into the forest if you are afraid of the wolves."

To which she adds this advice:

"If another dancer start to dance better than you, then you must work harder and harder so that you dance better than her."

The secret of Danilova's success lies in the fact that she is never satisfied with her own performance, but will always find some difficulty to be overcome, some fault to be corrected, in her constant striving towards an ideal of perfection not easy of attainment.

I

Chapter XIV

DANILOVA THE DANCER

ALEXANDRA DANILOVA is not only a great *ballerina* —she is the last direct descendant of the great Russian *ballerine* of the past—Istomina, Andreyanova, Kshesinskaya, Pavlova, Karsavina—most of whose names were world famous. Danilova's contemporaries, unfortunately, though equally great dancers and renowned in their native land, are quite unknown outside Russia, with the possible exception of Marina Semenova (a fellow pupil of Danilova), who in 1936 was allowed to visit Paris and give two performances at the Opéra, with Serge Lifar. This enforced severance of the dancers in Russia from those without is a great misfortune for the dance as a whole. Ballet undoubtedly reached its greatest artistic and technical heights in the Petrograd (Leningrad) and Moscow schools during the past half-century, and pupils in other lands must inevitably suffer from the lack of their tradition and precept. On the other hand, the dancers in Russia are deprived of contact with the great modern-classical choreographers of the present day—Massine, Balanchine, and Nijinska—all of whose work is far in advance of that of their contemporaries in the U.S.S.R.

Danilova, then, is our only true Russian *ballerina* at the present time, for though her friend and rival, Alicia Markova, shows strong traces of the Russian tradition in which she was educated by Diaghilev, she was never actually in Russia, while all the other leading *danseuses*, of whatever nationality, are pupils of the dance studios of Paris, London, or New York.

It may seem at first sight that lack of contact with the Russian schools is not a matter of great importance, but a more careful study of the results of both types of training will lead to the conclusion that it does produce a very different type of dancer.

Briefly, then, the facts are these: In the Imperial Ballet School (afterwards the Choreographic Technicum), the pupils were votaries of Terpsichore to a degree which children attending daily or twice-weekly classes can never attain. They were subjected to an almost conventual discipline, the object of which was to perfect them in everything appertaining to their chosen career, and, as the curriculum took from nine to ten years, no dancer could join the State Ballet until the age of seventeen, or more usually, eighteen years. The pupils were taught that classical technique is not an end in itself but only the means to an end, that just as a musician must master the technique of his instrument before he can play it, so the dancer must acquire technique in order that the disciplined body may have adequate means of expression for the moods and emotions of the roles to be interpreted. Dancers trained outside Russia do not share these ideas to any great extent, since in many cases their artistic training has been confined to classes in the dance studio in the intervals of their regular education, while owing to the fact that they frequently live at home with their parents, the atmosphere of an institution, where everything is directed to one particular end, is denied them.

The greatest disadvantage of this divided type of training is that the pupil is apt to confuse the terms "technique" and "dance", and to imagine that the possessor of a strong technique is of necessity a good dancer. This mistake is not wholly the fault of either teacher or pupil, but it is the result of the unfortunate absence of an all-round system of artistic education for the would-be dancer. These pupils often manage to learn in three or four years the amount of technique which in Russia would have been spread over nine or ten years of intensive study, with the result that they have by no means digested the learning which they have acquired. They frequently leave the studio for the stage when only thirteen or fourteen years old, and the result of this precipitation is seen in their dancing. They are anxious to impress the audience by their technical rather than by their artistic ability. They will deliberately accentuate the difficulties of a difficult movement in order that the public may notice and applaud their efforts, not realising that by so doing they are breaking the continuity of the ballet as well as the spell which it casts over the audience. No dancer in Russia would dare so to sin against artistic integrity! In this respect an article in the *Times* of June 24th, 1911, is worth quoting:

"The Russians in fact have so long since brought their technique of dancing, their command of their limbs and bodies, their instinct for balance, for energy without exertion to the highest point, that they have been able to develop the art for which that technique exists—namely, the conveyance of choreographic ideas. Russian ballet-dancing never for one moment escapes from its subjection to ideas—and, moreover, to artistic ideas, ideas, that is, conceived at a high pitch of emotional intelligence."[1]

An episode which fitly illustrates this contention occurred not long ago in the Ballet Russe de Monte Carlo. A young soloist, trained in America and in Paris, was allowed on a special occasion to dance one of Danilova's roles, and Danilova herself coached her very carefully in the part. The girl was surprised to discover that the choreography was much more difficult than she had expected to find it, and later complained to one of her friends: "You know, I had no idea that it would be so hard to dance. When Danilova does it, it looks quite easy!"

She is not alone in her misapprehension, for Danilova always dances so spontaneously and so easily that we get no hint of the long hours of toil and effort by which this ease has been acquired. It is only after we have seen some other dancer replace her in one of her special roles, and then see Danilova once more, that we realise the full extent of her technical ability and the consummate ease with which she performs evolutions which other dancers seem to find difficult. There are, of course, certain movements which do not come easily to her, notably the thirty-two *fouettés*, a spectacular trick much beloved of young dancers, though she can, and does, perform them. Neither does she concentrate upon turning numberless *pirouettes* in an *adage*, being quite content with the classical two. Perhaps she remembers the story of Semenov, who on one occasion, when his wife, Marina Semenova, exceeded that number, deliberately unturned her until only the required two remained.[2]

Danilova's artistic range is so wide that she can dance almost everything from the great classical ballets to purely national and character dances. She has made each type of dance completely her own, and, moreover, in no two ballets does she employ the same style or appear to be the same person, for she is always able to submerge herself in the role that she is dancing. Thus, her personality seems ever changing, and we see at the same performance not one, but many, Danilovas. Compare, for instance, the softly-flowing movements of her tragic Odette,

[1] Reprinted as Appendix B in *The Diaghilev Ballet in London*, by C. W. Beaumont.

[2] Igor Schvezov, *Borzoï*.

the Swan Queen, with the cold sparkling brilliance of her Princess Aurora, or Sugar Plum Fairy, all of which are classical roles—but how differently interpreted. Again, notice the brittle, pointed style of *Le Beau Danube*, and contrast it with the rounded coquetry of *Gaîté Parisienne*—both the Street Dancer and the Glove Seller are professional charmers, but, as she interprets them, their methods are as the poles asunder. To pursue the matter further, we can easily recall her bewitching Russian Boyarina in *Danse Slav*, with her flaxen plaits and flying blue ribbons, and match her against the peasant girl of *Igrouchki*. Both are true Russian characterisations, but as different from each other as the Noble Lady and the Goose Girl would have been in real life.

Danilova's method of approach to her roles is very interesting and instructive. She says: "When first I receive a new role, I listen to the story and find out what century it is in, and then try to create the period, for the style of dance vary very much in the different period. For example, the eighteenth century was very artificial, and so in *Les Femmes de Bonne Humeur* (*The Good-Humoured Ladies*), all the movement, especially of the hands, must be very artificial, otherwise the ballet will be spoil."

"Then next I try to put myself into the character and to create for the part a personality such as the Swan Queen, the Street Dancer, or the unpleasant young girl in *Le Bal*, who leave her *fiancé* and go and flirt with another man, but when the part have not any special character, as in *Les Matelots*, then I just dance as myself. I like best," she adds, "the ballets where the role, she have a character of her own."

Danilova is possessed of an astonishingly complex stage personality, which is one of her greatest assets as an artist, for while on the one hand she reveals an extreme spirituality and feeling for the unseen world, she has also a clear comprehension of the hard facts, failings, and troubles of daily life, all of which she shows us, enlivened by her wit, and emphasised by her great personal charm. In addition, she is able, by her very force of character and individuality, to compel our attention and sympathy whenever she comes upon the stage. It is for this reason that she is not a suitable interpreter for the symphonic ballets of Massine. The personality of the choreographer is so much a part of these ballets that a dancer of strong individuality is bound either to disturb their architectural balance or to become null and void in her efforts to be purely symbolical, and Danilova, too great an artist to obtrude her personality where it was not required, on the only occasion when she danced *Seventh Symphony*, chose the latter alternative, and seemed to be moving negatively in space. The one exception was in *Choreartium*, where in the third movement she danced like Springtime incarnate, free and joyous in a very young world. Just so must Proserpine have appeared to Pluto, when she played in the fields among the daffodils! Actually, Massine himself prefers to use Danilova in his lighter ballets, saying that while she can dance any role, other dancers cannot dance this type of part, adding: "It is easier to be tragic on the stage than to be champagne," and it is as champagne that he visualises her, with the frothing movements of her frilled skirt to complete the illusion.

When a dancer is as versatile as Danilova, there will always be differences of opinion as to which type of role suits her best, and in her case the critics do not agree in the matter, so what hope is there for the general public? In Russia she was regarded as a strictly classical dancer of rather cold temperament, though even in those days she did also dance the Russian national dances. With Diaghilev she continued on the same lines, though her classical work grew gradually more emotional, and it is not until after the departure of Nemchinova from the company that we hear of her in a *demi-caractère* part; her first role of this kind being the doll in *La Boutique Fantasque*, and from that day, to Massine, she was "champagne" on the stage. This new departure did not go unnoticed by the critics, notably by the late André Levinson, who wrote that he feared that such roles would eventually spoil her gift for "lyricism", though luckily this has not proved to be the case. Her lyrical qualities are still present, even to the extent of appearing in her lighter roles. Further experience came to her while working with Nijinska and Balanchine, whose "modern classical style" appeals to her very much, bringing as it does, movements of body, hands, wrists, and even elbows to add to the expressiveness of the classical technique, and incidentally this type of work suits her much better than the symphonic plastic classicism of Massine. Danilova has also a strong musical sense, of which she gave evidence during her school days (though she never succeeded in playing the piano very well), and which is easily noticeable on the stage to-day. She is never at variance with her music but always so strictly "on the beat" that, to her audience, sound and motion have become one perfect whole, and they are seeing what they hear and hearing what they see.

"Never worry about Danilova; just play the music and she will always be exactly right," said Rachel Chapman, the famous accompanist and pianist of the Ballet Russe, to a nervous new conductor, and it is no more than the truth. There was once a performance in Monte Carlo where an unaccustomed *chef d'orchestre* became excessively temperamental during the "*Mazurka*" in *Les Sylphides* and, slowing down to give full value to his musical ideas, left the unfortunate Danilova poised for several seconds on one toe, where she looked like a bird suddenly arrested in full flight. The effect was beautiful, but it must have been somewhat trying for her!

Backstage, Danilova is quiet and pleasant. She keeps her dressing-room, her theatre trunk, and all her belongings in perfect order, and seldom makes complaints of any sort. She is even long-suffering when other dancers, as not infrequently happens, try to take away some of her "special roles", and it is only when she considers that they are going a little too far that she will, in theatre language, *faire scandale*—in other words, make a strong protest to the directorate. This, however, is rare, though on one occasion she was bereft of her beloved *Swan Lake* from March to December, and when at length she did dance it, in response to numerous requests from the public, her performance was hailed as "the event of three ballet seasons in Chicago."[1]

But she loves peace and dislikes struggles, and, in the words of Mr. David Libidins, the administrative director, who has known her for years: " Choura has a very good ballet character —she is no trouble at all."

Danilova has raised herself to the very top of her profession by her own unaided efforts, that is, by hard work and the strength of her artistic personality. She has met with many set-backs, the chief of which was the death of Diaghilev, just as he had set her feet on the path to fame, and the anxiety of Colonel de Basil to publicise his "baby *ballerinas*" at the expense of Danilova, particularly in the United States. In Europe, Danilova

[1] Those of the Ballet Theatre, the de Basil Ballet, and the Ballet Russe de Monte Carlo.

was too well-known and too much admired as an artist for this to be possible, but, to aid his project, de Basil banked on the well-known preference of the American for those who are "hoping to arrive" rather than those who have already established themselves, but in this, de Basil was definitely mistaken. The public, as a rule, is quick to single out real merit, however little they may know of the medium in which that particular artist works. Danilova and Massine were the successes of de Basil's first American season in spite of his publicity campaigns.

Danilova has a profound dislike for publicity stunts and "paper *ballerinas*",[1] saying that the proper place to be a *ballerina* is on the stage and not off it, and that her contention is just, the following story will show.

A certain young London typist, having read a number of books on the ballet by a popular English writer and critic, decided to go and see the Russian ballet, then giving a season at Covent Garden. Her mind was filled with anticipation of the "baby *ballerinas*" of whom she had read great things, they being for the moment the chief pre-occupation of the aforementioned writer. All went well until the last ballet of the evening, *Le Beau Danube*, when something unexpected happened. Massine's entry and "*Mazurka*" caused her to sit up suddenly and pay much more attention to what was going on, and then Danilova's entrance enthralled her completely! "Who is it? Who can it be?" she kept asking herself, and, when the curtain fell, she snatched at her programme and read the name "Alexandra Danilova". Overcome by dancing such as she had never imagined, she became furious with the writer of her ballet books.

"The fool!" she cried to her friends. "The fool! Can't he see that she is the greatest dancer of them all, and he never even mentioned her!" It is needless to add that she never again read a book or believed a criticism by that author!

In this connection also is the episode related by Danilova herself. One day, during one of the first Covent Garden seasons of the de Basil Ballet, she heard a knock on her dressing-room door, and there entered the three "baby *ballerinas*". "Choura," said they, "we have come to ask you a question, for

[1] A paper *ballerina*; one who dances much better in the newspapers than on the stage.

Press Photo Service, Monte Carlo

ALEXANDRA DANILOVA AND IGOR YOUSKEVICH REHEARSING ON THE TERRACE, MONTE CARLO, 1939

ALEXANDRA DANILOVA AND LEONIDE MASSINE IN THE FILM "SPANISH FIESTA"

there is something which we don't understand. Why is it that while we get all the good notices in the papers you get all the applause in the theatre?"

Time has answered them; they are no longer "baby *ballerinas*", shepherded hither and thither, but have been able to develop their own individuality and to make proper places for themselves in the ballet world.

Danilova attributes her success as a dancer to the excellent training which she received in the Ballet School, the artistic influence of Diaghilev, her own continuous efforts to improve her work (she takes lessons on every possible occasion), and lastly, to the fact that "there is some part of me which *must* dance!" People sometimes ask her if she is not tired of dancing and all the wearing routine of theatrical life, and to them she replies: "I love to dance, and as long as I can improve I will dance. When you no longer improve, it is time to stop."

There are many beautiful girls among the leading dancers of the day, but none who appear to better advantage on the stage. Danilova's figure, with its long slim lines, well-placed head, and small face, is as near perfection as possible for the theatre, while, in addition to these natural attributes, she possesses to the utmost degree the "grand manner", that air of regality and nobility which distinguish her as the undisputed Queen of the Stage whenever she makes her appearance.

Danilova has a following wherever she dances, but her popularity rises to its greatest heights in London, where people will stand for forty-eight hours just to see her dance. In fact, she and Massine seem to divide the audience between them, and the shouts of "Danilova! Danilova! Massine! Massine!" which follow the fall of the curtain are something which once heard are never forgotten.

One one occasion, the first night of a new ballet (I think it was *Coppélia*) the audience went quite wild with excitement and the curtain rose twenty-seven times before Danilova would consent to take a call alone. She has a trick of blowing kisses to the audience on such occasions which gives her admirers great pleasure and is very charming to watch, and the audience will applaud continuously in the hope of inducing her to acknowledge their enthusiasm in this manner.

The present century delights in comparing its great artist with those of the past. Every newcomer is a second Pavlova or another Nijinsky, a fact which is annoying to the majority of the dancers themselves.

"I would rather be the first Danilova than the second anyone else!" once declared Danilova, exasperated by foolish questions as to which of her predecessors she most resembled, and she was perfectly right. More than a superficial or even technical resemblance is required to reproduce any given artist. The writer once inquired of a former member of Pavlova's company whether Alicia Markova really did resemble Pavlova as much as the critics at that time declared that she did. "She is very like her in face," was the reply, "but it is the other one, Danilova, whose dancing has the same ethereal quality." A remark which serves to illustrate how many different attributes go towards the formation of any one dancer.

Actually there can be no second Taglioni, Pavlova, or Karsavina, since what distinguishes one dancer from another is a particular personal quality which cannot be bestowed upon any successor. In the same way there can be no second Danilova, since her greatness lies, not so much in the different and often highly individual style in which she interprets her roles, as in the spiritual quality with which she infuses them. This spirituality is the very essence of Danilova herself. It is the flame which illumines her whole being, transmuting her work to a level of artistic achievement which enables her name to rank equally with those of her great Russian predecessors.

Danilova is often regarded as the dancer *par excellence* of light and amusing roles, but, in actual fact, apart from those ballets which have no story, there are few in which she does not hint at a deeper feeling beneath the surface gaiety and at the tears which lie so close to laughter.

To her classical roles Danilova brings the style and tradition of the Maryinsky Theatre, that "grand manner" and polished technique which is slowly but surely disappearing from the Western World. Those who would see for themselves what was Russian Ballet in all its glory should watch Danilova in the great classical ballets, such as *Le Lac des Cygnes*, *Coppélia*, *Casse-Noisette*, and *Giselle*, and compare her manner of dancing with that style, or rather, lack of style, which is coming into being at the present time.

Chapter XV

FAVOURITE BALLETS

WHEN Alexandra Danilova is asked to name her favourite part, she always replies, "My roles are like children to me and I like them all," but, in spite of this, she does admit to a special fondness for the following: *Le Lac des Cygnes*, *L'Oiseau de Feu*, *The Triumph of Neptune*, *Le Beau Danube*, *Les Dieux Mendiants*, *Coppélia*, *Baiser de la Fée*, and *Giselle*.

Some of these roles she finds easy to interpret—in fact, "they always interpret themselves"—while others require much careful thought in order to make them interesting and sympathetic to the public. Such, for example, was her role in *Le Beau Danube*, which she much disliked when she first learned it in Monte Carlo, but which she has since made famous.

Of *The Triumph of Neptune* it is not possible to speak now, as it has not been performed since the death of Diaghilev. Those who saw it seem to have liked it immensely and would be glad to see it revived. It was the first ballet ever created for Danilova as *ballerina* and was one of her great successes.

L'Oiseau de Feu she has not danced recently, as it is not in the repertory of the Ballet Russe de Monte Carlo, a matter of regret, since it is undoubtedly one of her greatest roles. The story of the ballet is based on an old Russian legend, the Firebird, being a mythical creature of great power and strength who defies capture by anyone. In the opening scene she appears in the enchanted garden of Kaschei, the Magician, attracted thither by his tree of golden apples. While she is playing with them and tasting them, Ivan Tsarevich climbs over the wall unperceived and captures her. The Firebird is astounded and struggles wildly, but cannot free herself from his grip, and, in the end, becoming utterly exhausted, acknowledges defeat. She promises that, as Ivan has conquered her, she will, in return for her freedom, come to his assistance whenever he calls upon her, and, in token of this, gives him one of her brilliant feathers. Then, free once more, she disappears from the garden. Ivan meets with many adventures which end in his being taken captive by the Magician. In his peril the Prince remembers the magic feather and waves it.

The Firebird appears, and dancing a Slumber Song, sends all his enemies to sleep, which allows him to destroy the soul of the wicked Kaschei. The Firebird then vanishes, and the ballet ends with the wedding feast of Ivan Tsarevich and one of the Princesses whom he has rescued.

The most lovely part of the ballet is the *pas de deux* of the captured Firebird and the Prince, which, as danced by Danilova and Massine, was a thing of strange and weird beauty. The useless flutterings of the magic bird, her gradual weakening in the struggle, ending in the meek lowering of her proud head in humble acceptance of defeat, were all wonderfully portrayed, so that one rejoiced with her when, having been released, she covered the stage in a series of flying leaps, revelling in her regained freedom.

Danilova describes *L'Oiseau de Feu* as follows:

"The Firebird is bird with character, very strong, a magic bird with hypnotic eyes, but proud and heartless. When she have lost her freedom, she begin to feel, and afterwards she pay for her freedom and begin to help people. Her dancing must be strong and show power."

Le Lac des Cygnes is, of course, familiar to everyone. In this ballet, Odette, the Queen, is under a spell which only allows her to appear in human form for one hour each day, and so we see her first as a swan, sailing across the lake to the enchanted wood; then, a few moments later, having become a woman, she emerges from the trees and bewails her sad lot, until the Prince appears so suddenly as to frighten her. She starts from him, for she is afraid of all humans and their love. Since her enchantment many have seen, loved, and tried to free her, but they have failed because their love has never been strong or unselfish enough. Such disappointments have only served to increase her suffering, so, although she dreams of a perfect lover, she is afraid to face one in the flesh and resists the newcomer to the uttermost. But this Prince is determined in his pursuit, and fate aids him, for Odette is so lonely, so unhappy in her enforced isolation, that at length she listens to his pleadings, puts her arm about his neck, and opposes him no longer.

Later, in the *adage*, that great danced love-song, she still remembers her strange metamorphosis, and shows us all the agony of her loving human soul imprisoned in Swan's form. Then, after the Prince's dance, comes her own *variation*, her

"Swan Song", for what she hopes will prove to be the death of her swan's body and her resumption of life as a woman. But, in spite of her warnings, the Prince has been too hasty, and provoked the anger of the Magician, and it is she who must pay the penalty for his folly and return to her captivity, more sad and lonely than before. She takes her last farewell, a moment of tragic beauty, and then disappears into the wood, only to cross the lake in swan's form a few moments later. The Prince makes one last desperate effort to follow her and falls dead in the attempt. All is still and the vision has faded.

There is a quality about Danilova's performance in *Le Lac des Cygnes* which defies description, something almost supernatural, for the tragic Odette, bewitched Swan Queen, is not a mortal, but an inhabitant of that strange land which lies somewhere "Twixt a sleeping thought and a waking dream", and so perfect are Danilova's understanding and impersonation that we feel convinced that she herself is really a denizen of that twilight world into which she so easily transports us. This ballet actually affects Danilova herself very deeply, which is probably why her performance makes such an impression upon her audience, and the explanation which follows is based on a description given by her:

"You see, no one have ever loved her enough, and so they cannot save her; she do not want to be hurt any more, but she always believe them."

There are stories about Danilova in this ballet which sound like legends, but which are nevertheless quite true. One of her partners told the writer that on a certain date he was dancing in *Le Lac des Cygnes* with her, when to his amazement he noticed that as she danced she seemed to radiate light. At first he took this to be merely a product of the imagination, but later found that this radiance was also clearly visible to the whole *corps de ballet*. It is sometimes visible to an audience during a specially lovely performance. Many people declare that even after the curtain has risen for the next ballet, Danilova's spirit still remains in possession of the stage, weaving its enchanted way between the more concrete forms of the other dancers. This phenomenon has been observed by the writer and by her companions during certain performances.

Quite recently Danilova has added to her repertory the Ballroom Scene from *Le Lac des Cygnes*—*The Magic Swan* the Ballet

Russe de Monte Carlo calls it. Here we see her, not as the Swan Queen, but as Odile, daughter of the wicked Magician, who impersonates Odette in the hope of winning the Prince for herself.

Odile, while trying to dazzle the Prince by the brilliance of her dancing, deliberately copies some of the lovely lyrical movements of the Swan Queen. The role is an exacting one, since, besides being technically brilliant, the dancer must be able to suggest something of the swan-like movements of Odette as reproduced for her own evil ends by Odile. Danilova fills the role to perfection; her dancing is brilliant and she manages to infuse something strangely sinister into the more lyrical movements. We sympathise with the Prince in his infatuation, but we cannot help feeling that some evil force is at work behind the festal scene.

Le Beau Danube, next on the list, provides a complete contrast, for it shows us the human Danilova, deprived of all her eerie charm. This is a penetrating character study of a young girl who exploits every attraction she possesses in order to gain her daily bread. She is a fascinating, seemingly heartless, reckless little charmer, and the performance is sharply cut, brittle and sparkling, but with a deeper feeling hidden somewhere beneath the laughter. The Dancer enters gaily and performs her dance with such spirit as to attract all the onlookers, until a shadow from her past life rises before her. The Hussar in company with a young girl—what does he mean to the dancer? Was he her first love? Perhaps—but we shall never know. In any case, his appearance is a shock to her, for her gaiety drops from her like a cloak, and she attacks him violently with the most crude abuse, and then, turning faint, is carried, none too gently, to a chair, by her manager. Habit is strong, and her first thought upon recovery is to arrange her dress so as to display her shapely legs, but then recollection comes, and she bows her face on her arms and sobs, until, feeling the sudden silence around her, she turns, to find herself alone with the Hussar. He, angry at having the young girl taken from him, makes a half-ashamed movement of appeal towards her, and then awaits her response. For one second she hesitates, and then, with a gesture of infinite tenderness, stretches out her hands. One seems to hear her say: "You still love me? Then come back, and all will be forgotten and forgiven."

The *"Blue Danube Waltz"* follows, and the little Dancer seems absorbed in her unexpected happiness, but alas! in the moment of victory all is lost, for just as she stoops to kiss her lover, the young girl returns and the dream is over. The Hussar leaps up, the young girl seems quite bewildered, for the Dancer turns on her in fury and tries to tear her to pieces, until the Hussar intervenes, when with a gesture of despair the Dancer, realising that her rival is too strong for her, runs weeping from the scene. Perhaps, of all her lovers, only the Hussar could have saved her from her present way of life, but he has betrayed her again and her one chance of happiness has passed for ever. She does not complain, but when next we see her she seems harder and more reckless than before. The ballet ends with peace apparently restored, but our predominant feeling is one of pity for the gallant little dancer.

Les Dieux Mendiants is a charming little fantasy. A God and Goddess descend to earth disguised as Shepherd and Serving Maid. The little Maid lays a picnic table for a party of Nobles who are spending a day in the country, and she attracts some attention from one of the Lords. Meanwhile, the Shepherd appears and exercises a great fascination over two of the Ladies, who both insist on dancing with him at the same time. The dance finished, he turns to the Serving Maid and dances with her, which draws the wrath of the whole party down on their heads, and both are told to take themselves off immediately. They, however, remain where they are, and as the Nobles throng round to see why they do not depart, they suddenly throw off their disguises and appear as their true selves to receive the homage of the assembled company. This ballet provides Danilova with one of those contrasts which she so much enjoys. The first half of the ballet she dances demurely as the Serving Maid, with little outbursts of mischief when she thinks herself unobserved. Later, as the rose-wreathed Goddess, she rejoices unashamedly at the discomfiture of the formal Lords and Ladies who entertained a God and Goddess, unawares.

Coppélia, one of the oldest of the classical ballets now performed, is still a great favourite with the public. The scene is set in a Hungarian village where Swanhilda, the village belle, is becoming daily more annoyed with her *fiancé*, Franz, because of the attention he is paying to a beautiful girl who sits in the window of the house of old Dr. Coppelius and takes no notice of anyone. What they do not realise is that this girl is only a wax figure. It is the day preceding the village Fête. Girls and boys dressed in their best are dancing in the streets, when they see Swanhilda and Franz and suggest that they dance the "*Ballad of the Ear of Corn*", to decide whether Franz really loves Swanhilda or prefers the unknown girl at the window. They dance, but the ear of corn has nothing to whisper to Swanhilda, who runs furiously away. Later, chance puts into her hand the key of Coppelius's house, and so she and her friends creep in to explore, while at the same time, Franz, having found a ladder, is trying to get in at the window.

Act II shows the interior of Coppelius's workshop, which is full of mechanical dolls. Swanhilda and her friends play with these, and have just found the doll Coppelia behind a curtain, when the old man returns and the girls flee in all directions. Swanhilda hides behind the curtain, dresses herself in Coppelia's clothes, and takes her place in the chair. Meanwhile, Franz climbs through the window and is captured and drugged by Coppelius. The old man then reads in his book of magic and decides to use the soul of Franz to bring Coppelia to life. He wheels out the chair and, making magic signs, thinks he is transferring the life of the boy to the doll. Swanhilda enters into the spirit of the game and pretends to come to life, but makes fun of Coppelius when his back is turned. Finally, she dances a Spanish and a Scottish *variation* to show that she has really come to life, and then rouses Franz from his sleep and makes her escape with him, leaving Coppelius to discover his doll (minus clothes!) behind the curtain.

The third act is a *divertissement*, the village festival and the betrothal of Swanhilda and Franz.

In the first act Danilova makes Swanhilda a gay thoughtless little tease, more child than woman, but altogether charming. Her dancing of the opening waltz, and the *adage* and *variations* of the "*Ballad of the Ear of Corn*" are among the most brilliant performances that she has ever done, the *brisés* of the coda being specially remarkable, not only for the way in which she performs them, but also because most other dancers find it wiser to omit them and replace them with something simpler.

The second act calls for miming rather than dancing, and Danilova's sparkling wit allows her to carry it off with a childlike simplicity which is wholly delightful to watch, and very

Photo: Wm. Rader, Hollywood

ALEXANDRA DANILOVA IN PRIVATE LIFE

ALEXANDRA DANILOVA AND FREDERIC FRANKLIN
IN "DANSES CONCERTANTES"

different from the laboured vulgarity with which it is sometimes interpreted.

The third act represents the festival in the village park. Swanhilda and Franz, none the worse for their adventure, dance their *pas de deux*, which is so much in the grand classical manner that we cannot help feeling that their adventures have changed them from irresponsible children into a very charming young couple.

Coppélia was revived at the Royal Opera House, Covent Garden, in September, 1938, especially for Alexandra Danilova, and it immediately became one of her greatest successes. She has everything which the role requires—style, technique, mime, sparkle, gaiety, and wit, and she combines them all in *Coppélia* in such a way as to make her performance a memorable one.

Baiser de la Fée, the last of her "favourite children", is also the newest, for she has been dancing it for only two years. It is a good example of Balanchine's modern-classical technique— *Hommage à Petipa* he calls it—and is very well suited to Danilova. The story is founded on Hans Andersen's fairy tale, *The Ice Maiden*, and Danilova dances the Betrothed of the young man, who, having been kissed when a child by the Ice Maiden, is pursued by her until she draws him down to her home beneath the lake. Danilova not only looks, dances, and acts like a young girl of eighteen, but she brings to the role a sort of elusive charm which is quite bewitching. To someone who remarked that she looked much more unearthly than the Ice Maiden, she replied: "That is as it should be. I am what he want and can never get!"

On November 24th, 1942, at the Opera House in San Francisco, Alexandra Danilova danced the title-role in *Giselle* for the first time in her career and thereby added another chapter to Ballet history. Her performance was so technically perfect, so moving, and, in the second act, so ethereal, that the audience found itself completely in accord with the critic Alfred Frankenstein, of the *San Francisco Chronicle*, who wrote: "No other dancer ought to attempt this part after the first lady of the Monte Carlo."

I myself have seen many Giselles; some of whom are best at the beginning of the ballet, some in the "Mad" scene, and others in the scene with the Wilis, but Danilova is excellent throughout. As the young peasant girl of the opening scene

K

she is as young and charmingly naïve as is, for example, Margot Fonteyn, while in the "Mad" scene, her tragic bewilderment brings tears to the eyes and a lump in the throat.

In the second act she is as light as Alicia Markova, but more wistful, more gentle and tender with her former lover, and even more ethereally evanescent—she is an illusion composed of mist and moonlight.

In partial explanation of this phenomena let us remember that the Giselles of recent years have all *descended* on the accent of the music, whereas Danilova, reverting to the tradition of the Maryinsky Theatre, *rises* on the accent, which being the correct as well as the logical procedure, gives an added lightness to the whole performance and especially to the second act.

Danilova has gained fresh laurels by her Giselle and has made another addition to the long list of roles by which she will always be remembered.

There will be no second Danilova, but is it too much to hope that after the war her country may once more open its gates to the rest of the world and send us, from that same Ballet School, dancers worthy to be her artistic successors? Such is the wish of the writer. It is also the hope of Alexandra Danilova.

Chapter XVI

DANILOVA HERSELF

PERHAPS the most difficult task of all is that of giving a truthful impression of the subject of this memoir, not as a dancer, but as an individual who has a life of her own, quite apart from the exigencies of the theatre.

To describe her appearance is fairly easy; Alexandra Danilova is five feet, four and one-half inches in height, of very slender build, with long arms, and the "most beautiful legs in ballet." Her face is heart-shaped, with round cheeks, straight nose, pointed chin, mobile mouth, and large, heavily-lidded, hazel eyes, the whole framed in thick, wavy, dark-brown hair. There are only two unusual features; one, the bend of the little straight nose to one side, which makes it appear in photographs to have a large bridge; the other, the power of the eyes to change their tint according to the colour surrounding them, or to the mood of their owner, becoming at various times blue, grey, golden, or, when she is sunburnt, a bright clear green, rarely seen and very beautiful. Her complexion is quite colourless, and has been variously described as being "magnolia tinted", or "pale moonlight" (la pâleur lunaire), and the effect of the brilliant eyes surrounded by this pallor is striking, while in summer her face burns to a golden-bronze shade which is extremely becoming.

"Why, you have the face of a mediæval madonna!" exclaimed the Russian painter, Alexander Yakovlev, when he called to ask her to sit to him for her portrait, and indeed, to those who are interested in art, Danilova's face will seem very familiar.

It is to be found in many paintings of the Italian Renaissance, particularly those of Botticelli and Fra Bartolomeo, as well as in the antique statues of the Goddess Diana; while the Madonna in the della Robbia plaque over the doors of the Church of All Saints in Florence might easily have been a portrait had it not been moulded some five hundred years ago.

Shortly after meeting Mme. Danilova for the first time, the writer commented: "You know, you are just like a Botticelli." To which she replied: "It is curious that you say that, for in Russia I was always called 'Cameo' for they said I had a classic face, but you are the first person to notice it since I left Russ."

During the ballet season in Florence in 1939, however, many people noticed this resemblance and it is now widely commented upon. In repose, her expression is strangely wistful and the mouth has a sad little droop, but immediately she begins to speak the whole face lights up and becomes mobile, changing according to the feeling aroused by the subject under discussion.

Danilova's voice, too, is one of her greatest assets, for it is rich in quality, low in tone, and well rounded. She speaks both French and English fluently, but has coined many of her own words in the latter, since she only learnt the language after her arrival in England. French, of course, she learned in the Ballet School, while in her nursery days she spoke German fluently with a succession of "Fräuleins" and can still understand it, but none of these ever seem to her to be as expressive as her native Russian. For Danilova is above all else Russian, and therefore, before endeavouring to describe her character, it will be well to consider certain Russian characteristics in general which may help towards a better understanding of her.

Maurice Baring in his book *The Russian People*, says:

"The Russian is adventurous and daring in the domain of thought, and of ideas; but in direct contrast, he is often distinguished by timidity, prudence, and want of initiative in the affairs of everyday life'. 'He will often display a horror of responsibility, a fear in the face of authority, a dislike of initiative, of striking out a new line; a blend of suspicion and fear of persons who seem ready to take responsibility on themselves and to signalise themselves by any act of initiative or independence', and a dislike of 'the man who speaks out and gives proof of moral independence and courage'.

"'Mobility and plasticity are characteristic of the Russian,'; from these proceed 'his power of comprehension, assimilation and imitation, a corresponding lack of originality and creative power, a great deal of human charity and moral indulgence, and a corresponding absence of discipline and a tendency towards laxity; an absence of hypocrisy and often, a corresponding lack of tight moral fibre, a faculty of all-round adaptability, moral and physical, and an unlimited suppleness of mind'. Just as the Russian 'will be ready to push his ideas to their logical conclusion, so in the field of action, when he happens to be adventurous and energetic, he will recognise no obstacles and no limits.   He will accomplish miracles, he will make bricks without straw, with gusto and spirit.   This is the strong feature of the Russian genius.   This is what distinguishes the Russian dancers from other dancers of genius.   A dash, a go, an extra flip of energy, a disregard of the inadequacy of the means at hand, a scorn of obstacles and difficulties, a desperate determination to accomplish the end in view'.   And this paradoxical temperament is balanced by their 'spirit of positivism and realism and their common practical sense'."

All these contradictions may seem very bewildering to those of other nationalities, but even as they do describe the Russian in general, so they are in some degree applicable to Alexandra Danilova, though in her, as in any great artist, they are at one and the same time softened and intensified.   For instance, she can adapt herself easily to foreign languages, but not to variations of temperature.   Since 1925 she has travelled all over the world for ten or eleven months each year, and is still upset by every change of climate, usually to the extent of losing her voice and being obliged to converse in a husky whisper, but, being a Russian, she recognises "no obstacles or difficulties" in her desperate determination to accomplish "the end in view", which, in her case, is the will to dance.   Laziness is a word unknown in her vocabulary, for she belongs to the "energetic" type; though she does find it necessary to rest for half an hour each evening before going down to the theatre to get ready for the performance.   But the rest is only for her body, since she frequently writes letters or sews her ballet shoes at the same time. But she really does rest when she is on holiday, for her greatest pleasure is to "lie in the sun and do nothing", though, on occasion, she has been persuaded into more energetic pursuits.

There is a charming story of her first mountain climb in Switzerland which shall be quoted just as she told it to an interviewer, who asked her what she liked to do when on holiday. Danilova replied:

"Usually I like to lie in the sun and not to move a muscle. Not even a little finger.   Just to bake—but last summer I go to Switzerland to stay with friends—and before I know it, I find myself climbing up a mountain with my precious feet put in beeg, beeg shoes which make me to walk like Minnie Mouse.

"Always before I have said what a fool these people are who

climb mountains—they bring no good to the world—they only bring grief to people who love them—or get stuck up on a mountain and make people come and get them down.

"But there I am doing it myself, climbing—and I liked it because I led all the rest—my legs are strong.

"And when we get on the top—Oh, I cannot describe it—it was like my first time to fly—it take the breath with beauty.

"And up there above the snow, among the rocks, you find flowers that do not grow downstairs among the crowded peoples.

"It is very important in life to see flowers that nobody else can climb to see, don't you think?"[1]

On her last holiday in Florida, she had another new experience, for her husband taught her to fish, and this both excited and distressed her, for she was afraid of holding the fish. One day, M. Kokich, who was being unusually lucky, handed her the fish one by one to be looked after until they went home. Danilova was sorry for the poor things being taken out of the water, and looked for somewhere where they would be comfortable. Eventually she discovered a hole full of water in the concrete surface of the nearby parking place, and here she deposited the fish. "They like very much," she relates, "and they swim round quite happy and I watch them, and then a man come and want to park his car. 'Not here, not here, please' I call out, and so he come over and ask, 'What is the matter?' and I say, 'Look, it is my feeshes,' and he say, 'I think I will feesh here and not in the sea,' and he laugh and go away. But it is nice for my feeshes and I am very happy."

The imaginative side of Danilova's character would appear to find its chief outlet in her art, while the more practical part is reserved for everyday life. This, however, must not be taken to imply that she is realistically practical in her home life, but it does mean that she is able to temper her imagination with common sense and to indulge her flights of fancy only when they will not interfere with her outward existence.

Her fragile appearance leads many people to believe that she stands in need of help and protection, though actually the reverse is the case, she being by nature extremely independent. On the other hand, she will value, remember, and often take, advice

[1] From an interview by "Candide"—*Daily Mirror*, April, 1940.

which comes to her from anyone whose opinion she respects, and will not hesitate to ask for it when she is undecided about any particular course of action. Her periods of indecision sometimes last a long time, more especially since she dislikes any attempt to dominate her conclusions, but often after days or weeks of thought she will make up her mind with extreme suddenness in the course of one afternoon or evening.

In money matters Danilova is reasonably careful, but she can also be fantastically generous; she has never been known to refuse help where she knew that it was badly needed, though she quickly loses all respect for those who, having borrowed, do not attempt to pay back at the earliest opportunity.

In general, she is gentle, kind, thoughtful, sympathetic and charitable in word and deed, but when upset can speak harshly and seem to be unjust, the reason being that her reaction is too quick for her to be able to understand the other person's point of view at the time; but it must be added that such outbursts are rare and are quickly over. Later on she will either apologise and ask forgiveness, or will become so sweet and gentle that it would be impossible not to meet her half-way and forgive and forget the offence.

Of course, many people are subject to rapid changes of mood but there are few who change physically as well as mentally, as is the case with Alexandra Danilova. The writer was with her in her dressing-room at the theatre one evening during a tour, and Danilova was very cheerful, talking and laughing about her doings during the day. She looked well and pretty and seemed quite happy. Before getting into her practice tunic she went to have a look at the stage, and there heard some news which upset her, for two minutes later she came back, a changed being. Gone was the gaiety, her face was set and shrunken, her eyes were a dull grey without any light in them, and her whole demeanour showed acute depression and weariness; all this was in less than five minutes. Again, watch her get out of a train after a one-night stand with another performance due in the evening. No one would think that the tired, white-faced girl with the little pinched face could have the energy to dance in a few hours' time; but see her after an hour's sleep and a good meal and you would hardly recognise her. She looks livelier and alert, while her very face seems to have rounded out and grown larger. She will certainly dance, and dance well, for though easily cast down, she has a wonderful power of recuperation which stands her in good stead.

But apart from fatigue and distress, she does always show that "infinite variety" which is so pleasing, and her moods are not in any way artificial or unreal since they are merely the changing facets of a many-sided character which, in its depths, remains always the same.

It is easy to recognise that Alexandra Danilova comes of good family and has been well brought up, for she has that sincerity and simplicity of manner, distinction of bearing, *savoir-faire*, and dignity, which is the hall-mark of the aristocrat. She is noticeable in any company without effort on her part, and while she dresses exquisitely it is always with simplicity and without unnecessary expenditure, and, in addition to this, she is possessed of great charm—"*la vraie charme slave*" as the French describe it.

This charm, while genuine and absolutely spontaneous, is also somewhat in the nature of a protective covering for the real self, and those to whom Danilova accords her friendship gradually come to regard her charm almost as they would a becoming dress, which, while enhancing the beauty of the wearer, seems to conceal, rather than reveal, the form within. For Danilova is most Russian in her division of her life into two parts, spiritual and material, and for her the former is by far the more important, or, as one authority has it, "The Russian believes so profoundly in the things of the spirit that he is apt to disregard the things of the body, just because they *are* of the body". But this division does not make life easy for her, since, like most Russians, she lives much more in a world of ideas, spiritual ideas, than do the peoples of Western Europe, for whom "spiritual ideas" are often synonymous with "moral rules", an aspect of the situation which would never occur to the Slav!

For this reason Danilova is a person of very few friends and hundreds of acquaintances, and it is characteristic of her to be seen about more often with her acquaintances than with her friends. Lack of mutual understanding in the realm of ideas is, of course, the reason for her rare friendships, and while it is true that there are many other exiled Russians both in Europe and America, yet it is equally true that the manner of their exile sets a wide gulf between them and her, since they are practically all political exiles, while she, who has no politics, was exiled for over-staying her leave of absence !

Thus driven into spiritual loneliness, and having learned from the disasters of her childhood the uncertainty of human life, it is small wonder that Danilova, always in deadly earnest where her work was concerned, threw herself heart and soul into her dancing, and then, in her free time, began to live only for the moment, enjoying everything which could distract her from her loneliness. It might indeed have been for her that these warning words were written:

> Ouvre à peu de gens ton coeur et ta maison,
> Car ils sont rares, qui, sans aucune raison
> Te cherchent pour toi-même, et en toutes saisons.

For Danilova, though quick and witty in conversation, is not a rapid judge of character, and will only too often take people at their face value in order to save herself the trouble of assessing them at their true worth. It is for this reason that she frequently falls victim to the type of person who hopes to better his or her social or professional position by being seen in public with a famous *ballerina*. These people are, of course, attracted by her outward personality, charm, and gaiety, while she, for her part, is sufficiently entertained by them to enjoy their company for a few hours at a time, though she fails to realise that they are making capital out of her behind her back by claiming to be her "greatest friends", or boasting that she "will not go any-where without them". It is possible, however, that even if she were aware of these manœuvres, she would consider the whole matter quite unimportant.

Life has used Danilova hardly, and the most crushing blow of all seems to have been her exile, with its consequent separation from home and family, as well as the loss of the sympathy and understanding she had always received from Maria Batianova. Naturally of a serious turn of mind, though with sudden bursts of mischievous gaiety, she became still more serious after joining the Diaghilev company, and in addition very unhappy, since, in her new loneliness, there was no one in whom she could confide or who took any particular interest in her as a person. Slowly she learnt to conceal her sufferings and to appear as cheerful and happy as possible, since, as she puts it: "It is not good to talk about sadness if you cannot make it better, so why do it ?

It is better to amuse and be cheerful so that people like to see you; and to talk only with friends when that can help." Having arrived at this conclusion, she set herself resolutely to carry it into execution, and thus was born the gay and witty Danilova whom we see to-day.

Being able so to discipline her outward self, she developed an intense dislike of those who allow themselves to be upset if they have a headache, or who go about expecting sympathy for some imaginary ailment or grievance, saying that it is unnecessary to allow oneself to be disturbed by such trifles. Circumstances have also conspired to save her from the "bondage of things", although the process has been painful to one who is such an admirer of the beautiful, but, as she truly says: "When you have lost two homes, you do not care to lose any more." She now limits her household purchases to essentials and takes care that these are of no great value.

But, while thus changing her outer self, the inner Danilova remains unchanged, and it is this quiet and serious Danilova whom her intimate friends know and love. They like to discuss with her those things which mean so much to them and to her; they try to make her happy and to let her feel that they love and understand her. They make no demands upon her, and she makes none upon them, only asking that they continue to understand her. They pay her few compliments and make no silly fulsome speeches, and she is glad to rest in the security of their sincerity and affection.

Whether Danilova be beautiful or no is a matter of individual opinion, for though she has the profile of a Grecian statue and the face of an Italian Madonna, her actual beauty depends on something far more subtle—the illumination of all her being by a light from within. This flame of her spirit invests her every word and action with such a quality of beauty that when she leaves a room it is as though she had taken the light with her. What wonder then that she attracts all who come within her orbit? The only wonder is that with all the admiration she receives she has remained so simple, sincere, and unspoilt.

She cannot be ignorant of her attraction, but she is utterly unaware of the profound depth of feeling which she arouses. She has no great opinion of herself and accepts all homage as a tribute to her art. But to those who feel drawn to her, she seems:

"Such stuff as dreams are made of"—a revelation of that hidden beauty which they have always faintly apprehended and sought—a

> "Dim vision of the flashing, perfect face
> Divinely fugitive, that haunts the world"

Of such is Alexandra Danilova.

Appendix A

DANILOVA AND THE CRITICS

THE following selections have been made, not only for their commendation or criticism of Danilova's work, but also because they do give a definite impression of her dancing in those ballets which are not in her present repertory.

LES SYLPHIDES (Paris, 1925)

"Quant aux variations féminines, j'ai découvert sans peine dans le corps de ballet des éléments capables de faire beaucoup mieux; faute d'étoile, faute de première danseuse, un sujet comme Mlle. Danilova est tout désigné à les remplacer. Cette 'belle ténébreuse' à l'allure si poétique, n'ayant pas encore perdu cet air de noblesse et de pudeur qu'elle tient de l'école ci-devant impériale, semble, malgré quelque mollesse, d'avoir l'étoffe d'une bonne danseuse. Elle me rappelle tant soit peu Karsavina à vingt ans. L'obliger à remplacer la robuste Nemchinova dans 'Matelots', c'est de gâcher ses dons de lyrisme et de 'lié', elle s'en tire, mais à son détriment."

ANDRÉ LEVINSON, *La Danse d'Aujourd'hui*.

LE TRIOMPHE DE NEPTUNE (London, 1936)

"Besides the Transformation Scene, which gave everyone a chance, there was a scene in a Frozen Forest with a flying ballet, and another in Cloudland that took one back appropriately to *Sylphides*, with Danilova, Tchernicheva, Lifar, and the rest of them in their most classical mood. It was Danilova's evening as much as anyone's—the first big part she had created, and the occasion of her official admission to the rank of Prima Ballerina."

W. A. PROPERT, *The Russian Ballet in Western Europe*, 1921–29.

LE TRIOMPHE DE NEPTUNE (Paris, 1937).

"Mlle. Danilova, brune à la pâleur lunaire, remplit le rôle de la fée avec une grâce moelleuse, voire un peu molle."

ANDRÉ LEVINSON, *La Danse d'Aujourd'hui*.

ODE (London, 1928).

"Another number might be likened to an elegy. I am thinking of a *pas de deux* in which the dancers (Danilova and Massine) jointly upheld, each with one upraised hand, a slender, horizontal pole, from the first and last third of which was suspended a length of gauze, a little higher than a man, and about twice the breadth of his body. This device was like two straight curtains with a gap between them equal to the width of one. A number of beautiful effects were achieved when the dancers danced behind the gauze, which invested them with an ectoplasmic quality, or else appeared alternately in the open space, so that a solid form danced with a shadowy one; sometimes their arms alone curved and crossed in the intervening space."

CYRIL W. BEAUMONT, *The Diaghilev Ballet in London.*

"Concerning *Ode*, the audience was left a little too much in the dark. How was it to know that Lomonosoff, to whom the text was ascribed, was a poet in the reign of the Empress Elizabeth of Russia, that Lifar's costume was that of a seminarist of the period, and that the crinolines were equally 'right'? . . . But the choreography of Massine was extraordinarily good. Lifar, as the 'Pupil of Nature,' was provided with splendid opportunities and made the most of them. . . . There was also a beautiful dance for Mlle. Danilova. . . . The main scene of *Ode*, with its soft-hued background and the dancers in pure white before it, is one to be remembered long afterwards as a feast of beauty in movement."

EDWIN EVANS, *The Dancing Times*, August, 1928.

APOLLON MUSAGÈTE, (Paris, 1928).

"Ce splendide athlete [Serge Lifar] est aussi un beau danseur qui saute, bat, tourne en l'air et à terre avec une robuste élégance. Et quand il supporte de son bras tendu le groupe des trois Muses placées sur la pointe en un triple arabesque, sa vigeur assure la beauté d'un 'équilibre' aussi insolite. Malgré sa raie à la garçonne, Danilova est, dans une tunique à la grecque, qui a remplacé le 'tutu', la Muse par excellence."

ANDRÉ LEVINSON, *Les Visages de la Danse.*

LES DIEUX MENDIANTS (London, 1928).

"Sir Thomas had, with great skill, strung together a chaplet of perfectly matched pearls from the Handel treasury, while Balanchine had disguised himself quite effectually, and would have passed for Fokine anywhere. Danilova was a perfect Fragonard Goddess, and if Woizikovsky couldn't look god-like, he at least danced as a ballet god should."

W. A. PROPERT, *The Russian Ballet in Western Europe*, 1921-29.

LE BAL, 1929.

"La douce Danilova, que M. Balanchine, exécuteur des hautes œuvres chorégraphiques, soumet à la question en lui liant les genoux et en lui cassant les pointes, s'en tire courageusement et remporte sa revanche aux côtés de M. Woizikovsky dans les gigues et sarabandes des *Dieux Mendiants*, sur du Haendel, donnés le même soir."

ANDRÉ LEVINSON, *Les Visages de la Danse.*

"The choreography was lively, muscular, and pretty—but not inspiring, though the *pas de deux* of Dolin and Danilova, who danced very well indeed, and the Tarantella of Lipkovska and Lifar were excellent pieces."

L. LOPOKOVA.

LE BEAU DANUBE and LES MATELOTS (Paris, 1933).

"Matelot ou hussard, M. Massine se dépensa beaucoup, mais c'est à Mme Danilova que revient la palme; aussi jeune que ses plus jeunes émules, elle détailla avec la même netteté les emboîtés et temps de pointe de la fiancée du matelot que la cascadante coda du *Danube Bleu.*"

ANDRÉ LEVINSON, *Les Visages de la Danse.*

BEACH (Paris, 1933)

"Se trouvaient en tête de la distribution M. David Lichine, qui force tant soit peu ses rares qualités d'élévation et de parcours, et Mlle Danilova, ravissante à voir sus le maillot blanc à monogramme; elle s'est montrée l'intermédiaire rêvée entre la beauté classique et la ligne moderne."

ANDRÉ LEVINSON, *Les Visages de la Danse.*

NOCTURNE (London, 1933)

"David Lichine scored a small triumph in *Nocturne*, both as choreographer and for his interpretation of the part of Puck. This is the first ballet which he has arranged. It is the story of Titania, Oberon, Puck, Bottom, and the fairies from *A Midsummer Night's Dream*, set to music by Rameau. Lichine evidently has a very remarkable sense of design, and one or two of his tableaux when Danilova as Titania and Massine as Oberon were carried *en arabesque* off the stage were very striking . . . Danilova was an ideal Titania, and in spite of a troublesome ankle danced brilliantly and the part of Oberon fitted Massine like a glove."

THE SITTER OUT, *The Dancing Times*, September, 1933.

LA BOUTIQUE FANTASQUE (New York, 1935).

"The third bill contained Massine's *La Boutique Fantasque*. It gave us the pleasure of seeing Alexandra Danilova for the first time this season, and a pleasure it was. Her Can-Can with Massine as a partner leaves nothing to be desired. A classic dancer *par excellence*, she has a fine sense of humour which she brings into play. Her 'classic' legs of a true ballerina (Danilova is the only one in the troupe who can claim this title) looked more beautiful than ever in the several *grands développés à la seconde* which she had an opportunity to do. The split with which she finishes the Can-Can was precise and effortless and beautiful of line. The *pas de deux* with Massine in the second part of the ballet was dexterous, lithesome, and exceedingly pleasing to the eye."

A. CHUJOY, *American Dancer*, November, 1935.

SWAN LAKE (New York, 1936)

"Though *Swan Lake*, music by Tchaikovsky, was a dull affair, woven along the unvarying fairy tales beloved of the ballet makers, it was distinguished by the extraordinary dancing of Alexandra Danilova. During the last two visits of the Monte Carlo Ballet we have become accustomed to hearing mainly of Baronova and Toumanova. This is not right, fine as these performers are. The best dancer in the troupe is Danilova. Whatever role she is given to dance she dances it superlatively well and with a keen understanding of its mimic implications. Her adagio in the *Swan Lake* was a miracle of balance, of grace, and of lightness. To see her rising to an arabesque was to bring conversion to the most stubborn of ballet atheists."

JOSEPH ARNOLD KAYE, *American Dancer*, June, 1936.

DANILOVA IN SEVERAL ROLES (New York, 1936)

"Speaking now of dancers, I am pleased to single out Alexandra Danilova for whom the past season has been a remarkably successful one. The revival of *Swan Lake* and *Firebird* has brought to the fore this very talented ballerina in two of her best roles. I doubt whether there is any other dancer in de Basil's company who could replace Danilova in these ballets. *Swan Lake* is, of course, her most brilliant work, and she reminds me of Karsavina in it, which is saying a great deal.

"Other outstanding roles of Danilova's are: 'The Firebird', the 'Street Dancer' (*Beau Danube*), the 'Can-Can Dancer' in *Boutique Fantasque*, the 'Ballerina' in *Petrouchka*, in *Choreartium* and *Danse Slave*. It is not a coincidence that Danilova's most successful roles are those of dancers, or in ballets where dancing is the primary consideration, for Danilova is first, last, always—a dancer."

A. CHUJOY, *American Dancer*, June, 1936.

DANILOVA IN SEVERAL ROLES (London, 1937)

"Nevertheless, to one member of the audience at any rate the outstanding feature of the evening was Danilova's dancing. Seeing her again after a year's interval one is struck afresh by her consummate mastery of every detail. Her precision, her neatness, her verve are beyond all praise. Above all, she gives an impression of certainty that is most delightful; it is impossible to imagine for one moment that she could make a careless movement or an ill-timed gesture."

Morning Post, July 1st, 1937.

THE GOOD HUMOURED LADIES (London, 1937)

"Who could fail to respond to *The Good Humoured Ladies* when Scarlatti sets the tune and Danilova leads the fun? This admirable ballerina seems to get as much delight herself out of Mariuccia, the naughty maid, as she gives; and to see her lay that alfresco table and join the contingent revelry is to understand why, after all these years, Goldoni is still remembered."

H. H., *Observer*, July 11th, 1937.

SWAN LAKE (London, 1937)

"*Swan Lake*, given by the de Basil Company at Covent Garden last night, is in every repertoire, and all too often its pure classicism has become influenced by the romantic 'Sylphides' which was, in fact, a revolt from the older work. There is a very sharp distinction in style.

"There are more obviously technical performers, but no one to-day who gives a more artistic interpretation than Danilova or who reveals the essential style of the work more completely. It was difficult to believe that this regal ballerina was the mischievous 'soubrette' of the night before. She received continual applause and a real ovation at curtain fall."

Daily Telegraph, July 14th, 1937.

"The abbreviated version of *Le Lac des Cygnes*, which is all that the Russian Ballet allows us to see of Tchaikovsky's finest ballet, was revived at Covent Garden Theatre last night. . . . Yet we ought not to be deprived of the chance of seeing so fine an 'Odette' as Mme. Danilova, also in the complementary part of 'Odile'. The loss to the programme of some modern triviality would, in comparison with our gain, be a small matter. The dancing of the Swan Queen in what is, properly speaking, the second act of the ballet, is, however, one of the supreme tests of a ballerina. The performance given by Mme. Danilova last night was expert in its nobility. The slow development of her *arabesques* and that assurance of grace that raises this kind of dancing far above the plane of mere gymnastics. She was admirably partnered by M. Petroff."

The Times, July 14th, 1937.

L'Oiseau de Feu

"*L'Oiseau de Feu*, which terminated the proceedings, remains on the heights throughout alike as regards choreography, music, and execution. Danilova danced with that lovely precision which gives me, at any rate, unique pleasure."

F. T., *Morning Post*, July 21st, 1937.

"Mlle. Danilova's performance in the title-role harmonised perfectly with the music. Indeed it is hardly an exaggeration to say that she became an extra orchestral instrument. Her restless style of dancing was well-suited to the fluttering agitation of the 'Firebird', although she did not always convey that suggestion which the music requires."

Stage, July 22nd, 1937.

"In *The Firebird*, Danilova's evanescent style of dancing brought out the beauty of the elaborate music as much as it emphasised the fluttering agitation of the bird itself, while David Lichine's Wizard was as macabre as he could make it. Richly-coloured music, scenery, and costumes, contrived to make this ballet something more than a mere exhibition of virtuosity, and created for us a living poem."

Yorkshire Post, July 31st, 1937.

Symphonie Fantastique (New York, 1937)

"Alexandra Danilova, so strikingly prominent in the first movement of *Symphonie Fantastique* is the true prima ballerina. Her beautiful legs are like humming-birds' wings, so flexible and so fast,"

A. Vitak, *American Dancer*, December, 1937.

Coppélia (London, 1938)

"The venture proved entirely successful. The décor and costumes had the advantage of freshness and direct appeal and Alexandra Danilova's virtuosity made the heroine, Swanhilda, a creature of extraordinary charm and grace. *Coppélia* stands or falls by the dancing of the prima ballerina, and at Covent Garden it stands because Danilova is the dancer. Never has she danced better than in this prodigiously exacting role, her rapidity and elegance are extraordinary."

Daily Telegraph, September 19th, 1938.

"*Coppélia*, Delibes' three-act ballet, revived in a new production at Covent Garden, is principally a triumph for Alexandra Danilova. For combined personality, wit, and astonishing technical ability, she has no equal."

S. F., *Daily Herald*, September 21st, 1938.

L

"In the course of time there have been many notable Swanhildas. Was there ever one more fitted for the part by their genius than Danilova? Within a minute of her first entrance she had been everything from a born wit to a consummate mistress of dancing."

W. M. M., *Evening News*, September 21st, 1938.

"Mme. Danilova proved herself equal to all its demands. Her delightful sense of comedy, expressed in admirable mime, her finished grace, and not least, the charm which she throws, like a cloak, over her technical accomplishment, combine to make this a great performance."

Times, September 22nd, 1938.

"Alexandra was a brilliant Swanhilda. To all the technical ability which the part demands, she adds a delightful sense of humour and power of mime. She conveys so well without ever over-acting in any way, that spirit of mischievousness which is one of the characteristics of this young lady who was jealous of a doll. She thoroughly deserved the big ovation she received at the finish."

Dancing Times, October, 1938.

"This old-fashioned classic . . . should certainly be seen by all ballet students. Its many short *variations*, one after the other, especially in Act 3, *divertissements* frankly designed to show off technical proficiency, are amazing feats of skill and endurance alone, but when given the polished performance of a Danilova and a few of the others, they are an inspiration. Danilova, in marvellous form, with not a slip throughout the long, arduous role, had ample opportunity to display her sculptured *arabesque*, lightning-quick *relevés*, various turns, and much strong *pointe* work. Her miming as Swanhilda was surprising in its delightful playfulness."

A. VITAK, *American Dancer*, December, 1938.

"Wit, technical skill, and consummate artistry have united to make Alexandra Danilova one of the great ballerinas of all time. She is a dancer's dancer, for the fine points of her techincal equipment never fail to evoke sighs of satisfaction from those who recognise the flawless line of her body, the brilliance of her *batterie*, the phrasing of her movement sequences and her perfect reflection in motion of the qualities inherent in the music to which she is dancing. But Danilova is also an audience favourite, for she boasts that intangible essence known as sparkle. You laugh as she bats her eyelashes in *Igrouchki*; you fall under the spell of romance as she dances the lovely waltz from *Gaîté Parisienne*; and you find yourself believing in magic as she dances the role of the enchanted Queen of the Swans in *Swan Lake*."

WALTER TERRY, *N.Y. Tribune*, October 13th, 1940.

SWAN LAKE (Chicago, 1941)

" . . . The high point, not of the week-end merely, but of the present season's three ballet engagements[1], was the *Swan Lake* of Saturday evening, when Danilova, admirably partnered by Eglevsky, proved herself beyond question, the outstanding ballerina known to the Americas.

The unrivalled elasticity of her dancing and the harmonious gracefulness with which her whole body seems to take on dancing as its natural living element set her apart from all other dancers. They are the reason that her work exhales charm like a perfume, and why the poetical seems with her not to be an added factor, but a basic function of her technique.

She is furthermore the one ballerina we know who can transfigure the technicalities of dancing in the same way that Fritz Kreisler, say, transfigures the technicalities of the violin. . . ."

E. STIMSON, *Chicago Daily News*, January 6th, 1941.

[1] Those of the Ballet Theatre, the de Basil Ballet, and the Ballet Russe de Monte Carlo.

SCHÉHÉRAZADE

"The Ballet Russe de Monte Carlo last night gave the season's first performances to *The New Yorker* and to *Schéhérazade* at the Metropolitan Opera House, and lest there seem to be no element of novelty in this, let it be hastily added that in the latter work Alexandra Danilova made her first appearance here as Zobeide. The idea of this predominantly classic ballerina (when she is not being impish) in a role that consists exclusively of dramatic miming may be strange, but in practice it works out extremely well. Not for a long time has Zobeide been so real a person or half so interesting a one. It is a crisp, colourful performance that holds the attention even through the scenes of ensemble revelry that surround it, and with André Eglevsky as the Blackamoor to play up to such a team-mate, this old Fokine masterpiece, so often limp and dull in performance, becomes once again tense and exciting melodrama."

JOHN MARTIN, *New York Times*, October 13th, 1941.

CASSE NOISETTE (Boston, 1941)

"Danilova, always on her toes in any role, was techincally flawless from her *pointes* to her candy-pink finger-nails. Arms and hands fluid and graceful, not a finger arched amiss, knees taut and straight, and dance flowing through the instrument of her body as sensitively as music issues from a rare and rarely played violin."

MARGARET LLOYD, *Christian Science Monitor*, Boston, November 5th, 1941.

DANILOVA IN VARIOUS ROLES (Detroit, 1941)

"Miss Danilova . . . gave in fullest measure of her art during the four shows last week. There is certainly no one living who can quite compare with her. The balletomanes' thoughts turned inevitably to the great Pavlova for comparison, and by all accounts, Miss Danilova did not suffer by the parallel.

"It seemed that each successive appearance of the dancer presented fresh evidence of her greatness. Perfection was piled on perfection until it seemed that human genius could do no more. There is an effortless quality about her dancing which is a reflection of the vigorous training of the Imperial Ballet."

J. D. CALLAGHAN, *Detroit Free Press*, December 1st, 1941.

SWAN LAKE (Chicago, 1942)

"Danilova remains the finest Swan Queen we know to-day. She has the technical equipment for the part, the exquisite sense of pause in timing, the regal bearing and the essential quality of languor. More than any dancer I have seen since Pavlova, she captures the feathery perfection demanded of swan-like mime."

CLAUDIA CASSIDY, *Chicago Sun*, January 3rd, 1942.

GISELLE (San Francisco, 1942)

"No more astounding demonstration of what a ballerina can do for a ballet has been seen on our Opera House stage than that offered last night when Alexandra Danilova danced Giselle in the ballet of that name. When the ballet was presented last week, its revival seemed to have little justification, and, judging from the remarks overheard during the intermission, most auditors shared the opinion that it was dull, overlong and not worth the effort.

"But last night Alexandra Danilova reversed that opinion. The veteran ballerina enacted the role no less beautifully than she danced it. She won the biggest ovation scored so far this season, and the profusion of floral offerings which supplemented the applause seemed to indicate the performance marked some particular gala occasion, the nature of which had not been generally revealed.

MARJORY M. FISHER, *San Francisco News*, November 25th, 1942.

"Danilova made balletic history Tuesday evening (Nov. 24th) when she danced the principal role in *Giselle* for the first time in her life. . . . Danilova solves the problem of this old ballet. Its operatic style is dated and creaky, and it demands an exceptionally sympathetic personality in its name role to put it over. This it never had until Danilova took it, and Danilova made it a completely different piece from what it had been. Her exceptionally skilful characterisation, the magnificence of her technical command, and the fact that she has exactly the type of face and figure beloved of the painters and draughtsmen of Giselle's own period, all conspire to indicate that no other dancer ought to attempt this part after the first lady of the Monte Carlo."

ALFRED FRANKENSTEIN, *San Francisco Chronicle*, November 26th, 1942.

"The famed choreographer Bronislava Nijinska, who coached the dancer in her new role, was overheard saying that Danilova's performance in the second act was closer to that of Anna Pavlova than any she had ever seen, and Mme. Nijinska must have seen quite a few Giselles.

Dance News, January, 1943.

Appendix B

LIST OF ROLES DANCED BY ALEXANDRA DANILOVA

Particulars of ballets in which Alexandra Danilova has danced the leading role, with approximate date of her first performance.

Choreographer.	Ballet.	Company.	Date.
Marius Petipa	Le Mariage d'Aurore	Diaghilev Co.	1927
,, ,, and Ivanov	Le Lac des Cygnes	,, ,,	1927
Arthur Saint-Léon	Coppélia	Ballet Russe de Monte Carlo	1938
Lev Ivanov (after)	Casse-Noisette	Ballet Russe de Monte Carlo	1941
Fedor Lopokov (after Fokine)	L'Oiseau de Feu	Russian State Ballet, Maryin-sky Theatre	1924
Michel Fokine	Une Nuit d'Egypte	,, ,,	1924
,, ,,	Petrouchka	Diaghilev Co.	1926
,, ,,	Prince Igor	,, ,,	1926
,, ,,	Cléopâtre	,, ,,	1927
,, ,,	Les Sylphides	,, ,,	1927
,, ,,	Carnaval	,, ,,	1927
,, ,,	Le Spectre de la Rose	,, ,,	1927
,, ,,	L'Oiseau de Feu	,, ,,	1928
,, ,,	Igrouchki	Ballet Russe de Monte Carlo	1938
,, ,,	Schéhérazade	,, ,, ,,	1941
Leonide Massine	Zéphyr et Flore	Diaghilev Co.	1926
,, ,,	Les Matelots	,, ,,	1926
,, ,,	La Boutique Fantasque	,, ,,	1926
,, ,,	Le Pas d'Acier	,, ,,	1927
,, ,,	Soleil de Nuit	,, ,,	1927
,, ,,	Ode	,, ,,	1928
,, ,,	Les Femmes de Bonne Humeur	,, ,,	1928
,, ,,	Pulcinella	,, ,,	1928
,, ,,	Le Sacre du Printemps	,, ,,	1928
,, ,,	Le Beau Danube	de Basil Ballet Russe	1933
,, ,,	Scuola di Ballo	,, ,, ,,	1933
,, ,,	Les Présages	,, ,, ,,	1933
,, ,,	Gaîté Parisienne	Ballet Russe de Monte Carlo	1938
,, ,,	Bogatyri	,, ,, ,,	1939
,, ,,	Saratoga	,, ,, ,,	1941
Bronislava Nijinska	La Tentation de la Bergère	Diaghilev Company	1926
,, ,,	Beethoven Variations	Casino de Monte Carlo	1934
,, ,,	Les Biches	,, ,, ,,	1934
,, ,,	Bolero	,, ,, ,,	1934
,, ,,	Danses Slaves	de Basil Ballet Russe	1936

Georges Balanchine	The Triumph of Neptune	Diaghilev Company	1926
,, ,,	Jack in the Box	,, ,,	1926
,, ,,	Apollon Musagète	,, ,,	1928
,, ,,	Le Bal	,, ,,	1928
,, ,,	Les Dieux Mendiants	,, ,,	1928
,, ,,	Baiser de la Fée	Ballet Russe de Monte Carlo	1940
,, ,,	Serenade	,, ,, ,,	1941
David Lichine	Nocturne	de Basil Ballet Russe	1933
,, ,,	Le Pavillon	,, ,, ,,	1935
,, ,,	Les Dieux Mendiants	,, ,, ,,	1936
Frederick Ashton	Le Diable s'Amuse	Ballet Russe de Monte Carlo	1939
Pavel Petrov	Opera ballets	Casino de Monte Carlo	1932–33
,, ,,	Dance of the Seven Veils (Salome)	,, ,, ,,	1933
Serge Lifar (after Perrot & Coralli)	Giselle	Ballet Russe de Monte Carlo	1942

Also the following ballets which have not one but several leading dancers:

Leonide Massine	Cimarosiana	Diaghilev Company	1926
,, ,,	Choreartium	de Basil Ballet Russe	1933
,, ,, and Argentinita	Capriccio Espagnol	Ballet Russe de Monte Carlo	1939
Georges Balanchine	Jeu de Cartes	,, ,, ,,	1940

LIST OF BOOKS CONSULTED

Beaumont, Cyril W., *A History of Ballet in Russia.*
Beaumont, Cyril W., *Michel Fokine and his Ballets.*
Beaumont, Cyril W., *The Complete Book of Ballets.*
Beaumont, Cyril W., *Serge Diaghilev.*
Beaumont, Cyril W., *The Diaghilev Ballet in London.*
Levinson, André, *La Danse d'Aujourd'hui.*
Levinson, André, *La Danse du Théâtre.*
Levinson, André, *Les Visages de la Danse.*
Lifar, Serge, *La Danse.*
Lifar, Serge, *Serge Diaghilev.*
Lifar, Serge, *Du Temps que j'avais Faim.*
Schwezoff, Igor, *Borzoï.*
Calvocoressi, M. D., *Music and Ballet in London and Paris.*
Karsavina, Thamar, *Theatre Street.*
Lambert, Constant, *Music Ho!*
Pares, Bernard, *A History of Russia.*
Pares, Bernard, *Russia* (Penguin).
Baring, Maurice, *The Russian People.*
Atwater, Donald, *The Schismatic Eastern Churches.*
    also:
Back numbers of the *Dancing Times*, the *American Dancer*, and the *Dance Magazine*.

INDEX